SO-ACJ-239

DEFINED BY

SEEING YOURSELF THROUGH THE EYES OF THE SAVIOR

OTHER BOOKS AND AUDIO BOOKS
BY TONI SORENSON:

Master

Behold Your Little Ones

I Can't Go to Church

Heroes of the Book of Mormon

Heroes of the Bible

He Knows Your Heart: Inspiring Thoughts for Women

Redemption Road

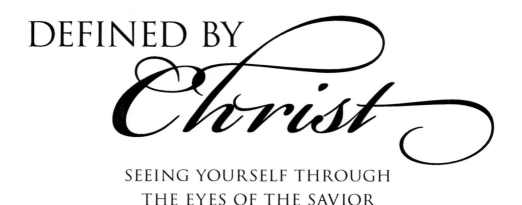

DEFINED BY *Christ*

SEEING YOURSELF THROUGH THE EYES OF THE SAVIOR

TONI SORENSON

Covenant Communications, Inc.

Cover image: Son of Man © Joseph F. Brickey. For more information go to www.josephbrickey.com.

Cover design © 2010 by Covenant Communications, Inc.

Published by Covenant Communications, Inc.
American Fork, Utah

Copyright © 2010 by Toni Sorenson
All rights reserved. No part of this book may be reproduced in any format or in any medium without the written permission of the publisher, Covenant Communications, Inc., P.O. Box 416, American Fork, UT 84003. This work is not an official publication of The Church of Jesus Christ of Latter-day Saints. The views expressed within this work are the sole responsibility of the author and do not necessarily reflect the position of The Church of Jesus Christ of Latter-day Saints, Covenant Communications, Inc., or any other entity.

Printed in U.S.A.
First Printing: August 2010

20 19 18 17 16 15 14   10 9 8 7 6 5 4 3

ISBN-13: 978-1-62108-583-6

For Bill and Margaret Pope, whose very lives define Christianity

CONTENTS

INTRODUCTION:
Silence the Pharisees

Go back with me two thousand years to a scorching day in the holy land of Israel. The air is so dry the leaves on the olive trees seem brittle. The sun is a ball of white fire, as brilliant as it is relentless.

Jesus has drawn a demanding crowd. He's tired. His throat is parched. He hasn't had anything to eat. Since the break of day, people have been coming to Him *en masse,* seeking His strength, His wisdom, His healing power. Among the crowds, as always, are the doubters, those who mock and accuse—that percentage who are always on Satan's errand.

The Pharisees in particular are clamoring to undo the good that Jesus is doing, to unravel the truths He is teaching and of which He is testifying. The word *Pharisee* derives from the Hebrew words *prushim* and *parush,* meaning "separated." These pious leaders have separated themselves from other sects of religious thinkers. They have elevated their own standing. They study the Torah and claim to believe its teachings, yet their lives do not reflect such belief. They stand apart from the humble Son of God, pointing accusing fingers, shouting insults and trying to destroy the One whose power and purpose is to save them from their sins.

It is under these conditions that Jesus turns to the Pharisees and asks, "What think ye of Christ?"

Now travel with me to another time and place. Go back with me a few years to my own house, nestled within the rise of the Wasatch Mountains. It's a humble home. I live in a community where Mormon pioneers planted trees and life is touted as good and simple—where the gospel of Jesus Christ is lived and nurtured and thrives all around me.

I'm alone in my room on a stifling summer night. My children are asleep in their rooms; drifting through the open window are the sounds of frogs and crickets. My head is pounding; my throat is dry. My eyes are swollen from tears that will not stop.

Fear surrounds me like so many lurking Pharisees. *Fear,* as the dictionary defines it, is a feeling of agitation and anxiety caused by actual or imminent danger. Fear is my familiar companion; it clutches my throat and strangles my thoughts.

I turn on the light and open my Bible. I bow my head and beg God to free me from these feelings, to fill my heart instead with hope and forgiveness—to guide me out of the darkness that surrounds me, even with all the lights turned on.

You see, after a quarter of a century, my marriage—my *temple* marriage—has imploded. I've discovered that everything I believed has been a lie. The marriage I never wanted to end must end. My life is in tatters. I'm certain my broken heart will never mend, but it's the pain my children are suffering that hurts the most. I ache to help them but feel helpless.

I plead in despair. *How, Heavenly Father, can they ever be mended again? Grant me the wisdom to know what to do and the courage and strength to do it.*

As my prayer deepens, I envision accusing fingers pointed at me. I hear the lies that are being shouted about me. And therein is the problem.

I believe those lies.

I've lost my own sense of identity—and in that process, I have allowed others to determine my worth and to define who I am. I blame myself for everything that has gone wrong. Because I believe the things I've been told about myself, I feel worthless, ugly, unlovable, incapable, hypocritical, stupid, bound to fail. And yes, even crazy.

My eyes open and, through my tears, I look down at my Bible. I read the scene where the Savior turns to the Pharisees and asks, "What think ye of Christ?" (Matt. 22: 42).

That question rings in my own ears.

My broken heart answers the one truth I've never doubted: Christ is the Son of the living God. In the midst of all my pain, I've never stopped believing in God. It's *me* I have a problem believing in.

Then something happens—something very private and personal, something I share with you only because of the transformation it has brought into my own life. I want it to do for you what it has done for me!

The words on page 1227 of my Bible seem to morph before my eyes. In my mind I hear a voice, but it's not asking, "What think ye of Christ?" Instead, I hear, "What does *Christ* think of *you?*"

Talk about fear!

A new kind of terror shot through me.

What does Christ think of me?

It was time to face the truth—not the truth about someone else, but the truth about ME. Was I really all the awful things I'd been told and had come to accept? If I was, then what? But if I wasn't—if I discovered that I was something different, maybe something more—*then* what?

Either way, it was time to put aside my own definitions—the opinions of others—and to allow Christ, and Christ alone, to define me.

Please forgive me for being so personal, but I can't offer you someone else's experiences; I can only offer what God has given me. I would not be sharing this with you if I did not want to help others who are hurting. I know the truths of the gospel are the prescription our wounded souls need to be made whole again.

My experiences and yours will not be identical, but I imagine you will likely identify with some of the feelings I had. Nor are my exact solutions likely to be the same ones you will choose, but I hope you will grasp the principles that guided my decisions. Most of all, I pray that you can be strengthened and find hope in the journey that God has led me through—hope enough that you will have the courage to take your own journey.

My journey began when my father died before I entered kindergarten. My mother, who was my anchor and my closest friend, was an alcoholic. Anyone who grows up in an alcoholic home will tell you that alcoholism exposes a child to things no child should be exposed to.

Abuse, for me, became a very personal word.

The gospel and its saving principles were not part of our home, but my mother did teach me that there was a God in heaven who knew me and loved me. The idea tugged at my spirit but seemed as fantastic as a fairy tale. That's not because I doubted God . . . it's because I doubted *me.* When I looked in the mirror, I saw someone who was worth no more than rubbish. I told myself that if I was worth anything to God, He would protect me and prevent bad things from happening.

But bad things still happened.

Then one day an elderly gentleman knocked on our door in Salt Lake City. He introduced himself as Leonard Grant Fox and told us he'd been assigned to be our family's home teacher.

I don't remember my mother ever allowing him inside our house. But I do remember him coming by on a regular basis, leaning on a cane for support and chatting with me in the yard. He told me my mother was right: God *does* exist. Brother Fox explained that God was my spiritual Father; He knew me and He loved me.

My only sibling, an older brother, nodded in agreement. He said our mother and Brother Fox were both right. God is real. He cares about every person on the planet, even me.

Really? My little heart burst with hope. I had sudden visions of a home that was stable and a mother who was well.

Brother Fox told me I could pray by just talking to God. When I was alone, I tried it. With the desperate faith of a desperate child, I approached God and begged Him to heal our mother, to provide all that our family lacked, to make things better.

In spite of my heartfelt pleas to heaven, circumstances grew worse.

And worse.

I ended up in foster care, and just when I needed her most, my mother was killed.

Decades later I can see how Heavenly Father used good and willing people to provide for me, to give me guidance and support. Some of those people even taught me the gospel of Jesus Christ. An uncle and aunt finally provided a home for me and managed somehow to love me when I was most unlovable.

In spite of everything, my faith in Heavenly Father and in His Son, Jesus Christ, grew. I was able to believe in *Them,* but it was nearly impossible for me to truly believe in *me*. While I approached life with determination, I lacked spiritual confidence. Worst of all, I defined myself by all the bad things that had happened and all the mistakes I'd made.

Along came college, a temple marriage, and a family. Church service provided tremendous opportunity for development, and my love for my family knew no bounds. But life wasn't what I tried to make it appear to be.

I wonder how many of us stretch our faces with smiles wide enough to mask the pain we hide. I wonder how many of us go through the motions—attending church, giving service, nurturing our families, learning and doing—while inside we feel empty, broken, doubtful, and even guilty for the way we feel!

That was me.

It all revolved around the old dilemma Stephen Robinson wrote so beautifully about—believing *in* God but not *believing* God.

I found myself teaching others that the Savior's Atonement was for them—but deep inside, I didn't believe that it was for me. For whatever twisted reasons, I believed I was not worthy of unconditional love, of forgiveness, of joy and success.

That's what can happen when we are convinced that we are just not good enough.

Don't get me wrong. I ached to feel the Savior's love and acceptance, but I couldn't. And I convinced myself that I somehow deserved all the horrible things that had happened to me.

Foolish me!

Like so many of us, I imagined that if I worked harder, produced more, reached higher . . . I would somehow earn the blessings of peace, security, and unconditional love.

Was I ever wrong! Simply by virtue of being a child of God, I was loved with a love that is beyond comprehension, a love without boundaries or conditions. But I didn't know that—at least not in my heart. I had the gift, but I had yet to claim it. My vision was clouded because I did not know what I am desperately trying to help you understand—that Christ says each of us is HIS, the greatest work of the greatest God (see D&C 104:14). We are children of God, who created worlds without number—and of all those creations, we are at the pinnacle.

If only I had understood that truth, I would have found strength to stand up for myself, for my children, and for my God.

My trials were not signs that I was unloved or unlovable. I know now what I did not understand then: adversity refines and strengthens us. It's not allowed into our lives to ruin us. It's there to make us stronger, more substantial in every way.

While I grappled with those trials, I found comfort in the scriptures and through prayer. I forged ahead; sometimes I stumbled, and sometimes I fell flat on my face. I felt that if I had enough faith, one day we would be the happy family I pretended we were. I had great hope that if I stayed close to the Lord, tried harder to love my husband and children, and more diligently served others, my faith would be rewarded and life would get better.

To those not really close to us, we appeared to be doing okay. But we weren't doing okay at all. Just as it had during my childhood, it only got worse. And worse.

Because I was relying on what *I* could do instead of what *God* could do, I wore myself out. In that exhausted state I believed the ugly, unkind things that were said about me. I'm sure some of them were true, but we are so much more than our mistakes and flaws. We are children of God. Yet through the darkness around me I could not see myself as His daughter. I allowed myself to be defined by my skewed thoughts and by the judgments of others—but not by Christ.

It was at that point that after all of my trying, divorce was my only option. Anyone who has ever gone through an unexpected, unwanted divorce knows the deadly freefall that comes with it. If I'd thought poorly of myself before, imagine how I felt then. In my eyes, I was a failure—an utter, absolute failure. That's how I saw myself, and I was sure it was how others saw me. And, by extension, I was certain it was how God saw me.

As much as I loved my Heavenly Father, I could not fathom how *He* could love *me*. I had disappointed Him. I had failed at the mission with which He had entrusted me.

Looking back now, I realize I was at my most hurt, but I was also at my most foolish. I was deceived by the screeching Pharisees inside my own head. President Henry B. Eyring explained that when we become convinced that God does not care about us, it can be very difficult for the Holy Ghost to help us remember the entire lifetime of blessings we have been given (see "O Remember, Remember," *Ensign,* Nov. 2007, 66–67).

President Eyring is right.

All I could hear were the shouts of the Pharisees that came at me like sharpened blades: *How could you have been so stupid? There is no future before you! Look at your past—you've never amounted to anything. You never will. Do I need to remind you of your mistakes, to list your sins again? Never forget that you are a sinner. Your children will not survive. You're too wounded to help yourself; how can you ever help them? You pray to God all the time, and what good has it done? There is no hope for you. No hope. None.*

Satan wanted to stop me from seeing the whole truth. He wanted me to continue believing the worst about myself and to feel only hopelessness and fear. He tried to focus my attention and resources on every mistake I'd ever made. He wanted to convince me that I had lost everything and that redemption was for others, not for me.

In one regard he was right—I had lost everything except for two things, and those two things mattered so much to me: my children and my testimony of Jesus Christ. I knew that if I was going to survive, I would have to shift my focus from mourning all that I'd lost and be grateful for all I had left. I was in the midst of trying to sort out the chaos when the question came: *What does Christ think of you?*

The answer is something I can't wait to share with you— because if you've ever suffered betrayal, disappointment, the pain of injustice, or the sorrow of sin, if you have ever felt utterly inadequate or an absolute failure, the answer has the power to change your life as surely as it changed mine.

Are you ready to face the truth—the whole truth, and nothing but the truth—about yourself? Are you serious about forging an eternal relationship with Christ? Are you passionate about living the gospel to its fullest? Are you really ready to live the life Christ lived and died for you to have?

If you are, then it's time you let Christ—and no one else— define you.

No matter where you are or how much pain you're in, God knows where you are, and His power can heal you. He can lead you out of the darkness back into the light. He is the mender of all things broken.

Looking back, everything in my life seemed broken—not only my marriage, but my family. My finances. My job. My home. My relationships. My self-image. There were moments I wished I'd never existed—not because I had problems, but because I had lost my spiritual identity. I had no clear vision of who I was or what I was worth in the sight of God.

My spirit was black and blue and broken. I had done all I could, and it just wasn't enough. It wasn't. I knew it, and I knew all of heaven knew it.

That is when I was hit by that sledgehammer query: *What does Christ think of you?*

For the answer, I turned to the scriptures.

I read of Alma, a man whose very purpose and worth had been *RE*-defined by his encounter with Christ. So had the lives of his cherished friends, the sons of Mosiah. In their youth they'd caused great destruction to the Church. They'd injured others. They'd disobeyed God's laws and broken their parents' hearts. But through repentance and the power of Christ's atonement, they were no longer defined by their pasts, by their sins and mistakes, and by the judgments of others. They were now defined by Jesus Christ, and they wanted nothing more than to bring others to His saving love and power.

After years of separation, Alma and his friends were reunited in the midst of unfathomable trials. Alma discovered why his friends had remained fiercely dedicated to the Lord's work, how they had avoided being pulled back into the condemnation of their pasts: "they had waxed strong in the knowledge of the truth; for they were men of a sound understanding and they had searched the scriptures diligently, that they might know the word of God" (Alma 17:2).

How had they waxed strong in the knowledge of truth? How had they become men of sound understanding? *They had searched the scriptures diligently!* Why? *To know the word of God!*

They had a sound understanding of who they were in Christ. To be *sound* means to be steady and secure. I wanted a sound understanding of my own identity. I'd spent my life tossed about by feelings—by the measure of others. That's not healthy or faithful. It was time for an eternal change. I determined to know the word of God so I could find out what it had to say about me and my life. I needed a blueprint to restore all that had been demolished.

At a spring 1986 priesthood leadership meeting, President Ezra Taft Benson talked about Lehi's dream and the meaning of the rod of iron, which represents the word of God. He emphasized that "not only will the word of God lead us to the fruit which is desirable above all others, but that in the word of God and through it we can find the power to resist temptation, the power to thwart the work of Satan and his emissaries" ("The Power of the Word," *Ensign,* May 1986, 79).

Satan was out to finish the work he'd started in our family, but here was a promise from a prophet! In the word of God I could find "the power to thwart the work of Satan and his emissaries."

I took that promise seriously.

Make no mistake. Satan is not out to destroy my family alone, but yours too. He's an expert at discovering the weakest link and worming his way past our thresholds and into our homes and thoughts and lives.

I once purchased a security system for our home to keep my family safe. It came with a variety of electronic devices to help ensure that no intruder could enter. It also came with instructions and passwords and codes that had to be studied and remembered. God has given us a similar security system known as the scriptures. They also come with instructions and information that must be remembered so that when we are being invaded, we know how to activate their truths and stop the intruder from entering our hearts and our thoughts and our lives.

In the same address, President Benson said that the "word of God, as found in the scriptures, in the words of living prophets, and in personal revelation, has the power to fortify the Saints and arm them with the Spirit so they can resist evil, hold fast to the good, and find joy in this life" ("The Power of the Word," 79).

Oh, how I wanted to replace the fear in my life with faith. The sorrow with joy. The pain with peace.

Down on my knees, with the scriptures opened before me, I embarked on a desperate mission of self-discovery. Right away the Spirit seemed to guide me: "If you want to discover who you are, you must first understand who God is."

That was the first of several important truths I learned—truths I want to share with you. Because they made all the difference in my life, just as I'm sure they will in yours.

TRUTH #1:
God Is Our Father

The Spirit itself beareth witness with our spirit,
that we are the children of God.
—Romans 8:16

Coming to know God is like looking in a mirror and seeing past the aging face that greets me every day. It's like seeing a spirit that resembles me—but instead of being constructed of decaying flesh and bones, it's made of unfailing light and joy. It's like seeing myself as God sees me: as His child—a child of infinite worth, one who is loved beyond measure. For years I had allowed life's cruelties and the world's lies to deceive me about God and myself. I was convinced that He loved everyone else, but certainly had to be disappointed at *my* performance—even ashamed of me. I was like a little girl trying desperately to please her father but forever failing. My heart swelled with love for Him, and I ached to please Him, but no matter how hard I tried, I believed He was always disappointed in me. Even my very best efforts never seemed good enough. No wonder my prayers were timid and pathetic. Foolish me!

Before I could make a new spiritual beginning, I had to stop focusing on what I *wasn't*, and I had to figure out what I *was*. I was more than an orphan. I was more than a single mother. My wake up call came when I realized that as long as I was focused on myself and my problems, I could not be focused on my Father in Heaven and His loving Son, my Savior.

Everyone on this earth struggles—even those who seem to have all the advantages. It's part of God's plan. It's how we come to the realization that we have to rely on Him instead of on our own strength. And it brings us to a realization of His merciful plan. Regardless of any disadvantage we face, our Heavenly Father can fill any void and can make up for all that we lack. He knows us better than we know ourselves, and His perfect plan can catch us when we fall and redeem us when we sell ourselves short.

GETTING TO KNOW HIM

How can we really get to know this celestial Father whose perfect love never fails? How do we begin to identify ourselves as His children? For me, it was on my knees.

Even though I'd prayed thousands of times—even though I'd read the scriptures and marked them up until they looked like my little boy's coloring book—I had never prayed a prayer like the one I did when I was at my lowest point: "Father, please help me come to know Thee." It doesn't matter how long I stayed on my knees or what the rest of my prayer sounded like. What matters is that the Spirit gently and lovingly led me to a truth that I wasn't expecting. It was a truth about myself—the kind of truth that truly sets us free.

The truth about me was that I lacked faith. What?

Faith.

My financial bank account had insufficient funds. In a similar but more important way, my spiritual bank account had insufficient faith. And it takes faith to know God. At first I was offended. Me? *Insufficient faith?* I must have misinterpreted. After all, I'd hung in there. I had spent years as an active Latter-day Saint. I'd served in every organization of the Church. I'd played the organ in sacrament meeting and helped dozens of Sunbeams learn to fold their arms and bow their heads. I'd been married in the temple. I'd cleaned the meetinghouse and shoveled snow from the parking lot. I'd mothered six children. I'd survived Young Women's camp and Webelos. I'd taught gospel doctrine. I knew how to bear my testimony in multiple languages. I could recite the Articles of Faith word for word. Silently, I'd endured ferocious trials. Didn't all of that indicate faith?

What I needed, I thought, was a *miracle*—not more faith.

I tried again. "Father, I'm not praying for myself. I am praying for my children. They are wounded worse than I am. I want to know Thee so that I can better help them."

Again, the Spirit whispered, "You need more faith."

"Okay, okay," I relented, "then give me more faith."

I wish I could tell you it was easy.

It wasn't.

That little tugging sensation tugged me to the ninth chapter of Mark. The account there records a typical day during the Savior's ministry. The Savior was often surrounded by multitudes of people who needed more faith, and on this particular day, Jesus is listening to an exchange between His disciples and the scribes.

Please read the scriptural account carefully, starting in verse sixteen. Jesus asks the scribes, "What question ye with them?" What happens next is instructive:

> And one of the multitude answered and said, Master, I have brought unto thee my son, which hath a dumb spirit;

> And wheresoever he taketh him, he teareth him: and he foameth, and gnasheth with his teeth, and pineth away: and I spake to thy disciples that they should cast him out; and they could not.
>
> He answereth him, and saith, O faithless generation, how long shall I be with you? how long shall I suffer you? bring him unto me. (Mark 9:16–19)

So here is a parent, desperate to save his suffering child. Already, the story spoke to my distraught soul. The story continues:

> And they brought him unto him: and when he saw him, straightway the spirit tare him; and he fell on the ground, and wallowed foaming.
>
> And he asked his father, How long is it ago since this came unto him? And he said, Of a child.
>
> And ofttimes it hath cast him into the fire, and into the waters, to destroy him: but if thou canst do any thing, have compassion on us, and help us.
>
> Jesus said unto him, If thou canst believe, all things are possible to him that believeth.
>
> And straightway the father of the child cried out, and said with tears, Lord, I believe; help thou mine unbelief.
>
> When Jesus saw that the people came running together, he rebuked the foul spirit, saying unto him, Thou dumb and deaf spirit, I charge thee, come out of him, and enter no more into him.

And the spirit cried, and rent him sore, and came out of him: and he was as one dead; insomuch that many said, He is dead.

But Jesus took him by the hand, and lifted him up; and he arose. (Mark 9:20–27)

Can you feel the impact of this story in your own life? There are so many lessons on so many levels for those of us who need to increase our faith in order to better know our Father in Heaven. First of all, we have to approach God. We have to express our need. We have to be willing to believe. Note that the desperate father said, "*If* thou canst do any thing." He didn't say, "Thou canst do anything."

And what did Jesus say to the father? "If thou canst believe"— *If* thou canst believe—"all things are possible." That was the message for me. That beautiful, humble, desperate father was an example of the strongest kind of man. He did not hesitate or argue; he simply cried through his tears, "Lord, I believe; help thou mine unbelief." When I first prayed to know God I suppose I wanted the veil to part. Instead, my heart came apart and I cried with the same words, "Lord, I believe. Help thou mine unbelief." I promise you that no sincere prayer goes unheard. With time, fervent prayer, and an increasing desire for more faith, I came to know that God is NOT a foreign being perched on a throne pointing an accusing finger at me. He never shook His head, muttering, "That Toni, what a letdown. I never expected this kind of behavior from her. She's really caught me off-guard." Foolish, foolish me. Even though I'd been active in the Church, even though I thought I had a testimony, I didn't know the One Joseph Smith called "the Great Parent of the universe" (*History of the Church,* 4:595). I didn't begin to comprehend His majesty, His might, His power. Most of all, I didn't begin to comprehend His mercy and His unbounded love.

ALL THE DIFFERENCE

Years ago Elder Bernard P. Brockbank, Assistant to the Quorum of the Twelve, explained, "Many believe that there is a God, many say that they know there is a God, but many do not act like they *know* God. There is a great difference in believing or knowing that there is a God and in knowing God" ("Knowing God," *Ensign,* July 1972, 121).

After my own spiritual wrestling, I understood that there is only one way to know who we really are: through knowing God our Father. And there is only one way to come to know God: through Jesus Christ. And there is only one way to come to know Jesus Christ: through the power of the Holy Spirit. I plead with you to take this journey yourself. Go get your scriptures. Find a quiet place where you can be alone with God. Pray. If you lack sufficient faith, pray for an increase of faith, and be willing to do whatever the Spirit guides you to do to receive that bounty.

This is an essential step. The Prophet Joseph Smith left no wiggle room: "It is the first principle of the gospel to know for a certainty the character of God" (*History of the Church,* 6:305). When declaring what we believe, he put first thing first: "We believe in God, the Eternal Father" (A of F 1:1). How can we *believe* in Him if we don't *know* Him? How can we believe in *ourselves* if we don't know who *we* are?

To illustrate this point, allow me to introduce two very different people. Seven-year-old Jacoby was a member of my Primary class. Jacoby is a tall, towheaded boy with enthusiasm that approaches nuclear force. One morning while we were all reciting the Primary theme—"I am a child of God. I know Heavenly Father loves me"—Jacoby began to spin like a top. As he turned in circles, his arms like spinning propellers, his voice rose above every other voice: "I know Heavenly Father loves me, and I love Him. I love Him! I love Him! I love Him!"

When he slowed to a safe speed I leaned down and asked him, "Jacoby, why do you love Heavenly Father so much?"

He came to a dead stop. "I love Him so much because He loves me so much!"

Jacoby was right. Heavenly Father does love us so much. We should all be spinning and shouting for joy.

So why aren't we?

Because no matter how much we do, no matter how much we give or how hard we try, every single one of us is occasionally going to fail. When we find ourselves scraping the bottom, there is only *one way* to pull ourselves back up—and that is with the never-failing hand of our Father. That hand is extended to us through our Savior, sent from God, to lift us when we are left for dead. Remember that when Jesus cast the evil spirit from the young boy, many looked and thought the child was dead. "But Jesus took him by the hand, and lifted him up; and he arose" (Mark 9:27).

Where the world sees death, God sees life.

REMEMBER

In the Doctrine and Covenants we are told, "Remember the worth of souls is great in the sight of God" (D&C 18:10). We are not told to *learn* that the worth of souls is great in the sight of God. We are not told to *understand*. We are told to *remember*. That can mean only one thing: at some point we *knew* our worth in the sight of God.

Now that you know Jacoby, I'd like to introduce you to Angela, a woman I met through a prison ministry. Angela is a slight woman, not yet quite thirty years old. She speaks with a thick Southern accent. One afternoon Angela told me that both of her parents had abused her. "I have no worth," she said, through tears. "I am who I am—the daughter of abusers." I promised her, "You are also the daughter of God. You can overcome anything to become anyone you choose to be." She laughed through her tears. "I wish I believed you."

I held Angela in my arms and prayed that her heart would be filled with the one truth that I pray your hearts will embrace: every person on this earth is a son or daughter of God. No matter who you are, no matter where you live, no matter what you look like or what you've done, God is your spiritual Father. Nothing can or will ever change that.

I won't pretend I understood Angela's pain as she pulled away from me asking, "Who is God? Really, who is He and how can I know Him?" I'm afraid my answer was both truthful and trite. "Pray. Read your scriptures."

She smirked. "It's that easy, huh?"

My heart broke as I compared Angela to Jacoby. Imagine the lives that would be transformed if we all realized that there is *nothing* more important to a happy, fulfilled, productive life than a relationship with God the Father.

The Prophet Joseph Smith taught: "There are but a very few beings in the world who understand rightly the character of God. The great majority of mankind do not comprehend anything, either that which is past, or that which is to come, as it respects their relationship to God. . . . If men do not comprehend the character of God, they do not comprehend themselves" (*History of the Church,* 6:303).

There is no overemphasizing what I have come to know through purging personal experience: the MOST important relationship we will ever develop will be with our Eternal Father. You cannot know yourself until you know God. In an effort to help Angela, I laid out some facts about our Father in Heaven.

A Few Facts

God is the great Creator. "The heavens declare the glory of God; and the firmament sheweth His handywork" (Psalm 19:1). Under His direction the sand beneath your feet was formed, the mountaintops sculpted, the ocean beds filled with water, the forests planted and nurtured. The sun and stars and moon were set in place by His divine direction. His creations are limitless. Believing in Him is not difficult if you're willing to open your mind and heart and eyes. The prophet Alma put it plainly: "all things denote there is a God; yea, even the earth, and all things that are upon the face of it, yea, and its motion, yea, and also all the planets which move in their regular form do witness that there is a Supreme Creator" (Alma 30:44).

God has a perfected body of flesh and bones. Joseph Smith was devout in clearing up the misconceptions about God the Father: "God himself was once as we are now, and is an exalted man, and sits enthroned in yonder heavens! . . . It is the first principle of the Gospel to know for a certainty the Character of God, and to know that we may converse with him as one man converses with another, and that he was once a man like us; yea, that God himself, the Father of us all, dwelt on an earth, the same as Jesus Christ himself did" (*Teachings of the Prophet Joseph Smith* [Salt Lake City: Deseret Book, 1938], 345–46).

We are the spiritual offspring of God, created in His image. We are literally children of God. His spiritual DNA runs through us. We were spiritually begotten in the premortal life—and, like any child far away from home, we can call and find a parent happy to hear from us, eager to listen to our joys and sorrows, and willing to help us. Elder M. Russell Ballard taught that, as part of His family, He is our father in a very literal sense—and that he yearns for us to return and live with Him (see "The Atonement and the Value of One Soul," *Ensign,* May 2004, 84).

Of all of God's creations, you are the greatest. God's creations are without number, yet His very work is to save each one of us that we might become as He is (see Moses 1:33, 38–39).

God is approachable. One day at the mall I heard a lost little boy cry out, "Mommy!" The boy wasn't mine, but I still felt that tightening in my chest and a desire to answer his call. Because I'm a mother, I instinctively wanted to rush to him and pick him up and dry his tears. Imagine, then, how fast our Heavenly Father whips around and comes to our aid when He hears us cry out to Him! He is mindful of us—of what is going on in our lives. He *wants* to hear from us, and He wants to help. As I have come to know God better, I've stopped *saying* my prayers and have instead learned that to truly pray means more listening than talking.

The Great King wants us to come BOLDLY to His throne. To pray *boldly* means to ask for our heart's desires—to pray expecting a loving God to answer. The reason most of us don't pray boldly is because we feel unworthy. None of us is perfect, and Heavenly Father knows that. He does not expect perfection from us—not yet, anyway. He expects our best effort, a full measure. He knows our hearts and wants to bless us.

God is merciful. His mercy is so boundless that He gave His first, His favored, His flawless Son so that we might be able to return to live with Him, to become like Him. My simple mortal mind cannot fathom that kind of mercy, that unconditional love, and yet I have felt it through gentle whisperings and answered prayers. He provides the mercy; we provide the broken hearts and contrite spirits. We repent; He extends mercy.

God is just. In the end, all that is wrong will be made right. In his final general conference address, Elder Joseph B. Wirthlin wrapped up this principle with a heart-stopping promise: "The Lord compensates the faithful for every loss. That which is taken away from those who love the Lord will be added unto them in His own way. While it may not come at the time we desire, the faithful will know that every tear today will eventually be returned a hundredfold with tears of rejoicing and gratitude" ("Come What May, and Love It," *Ensign,* Nov. 2008, 28).

God will never cease to be God. We humans sometimes think that *our* behavior alters *God's* behavior. It's not possible. I have a friend who has not prayed in decades because she believes her behavior has disappointed God. She's dead wrong. Our behavior does not alter God's behavior. He is the same yesterday, today, and forever. He's not moody, unpredictable, or volatile. He never, ever goes back on His word. He is perfect.

The most important thing we will ever do is love God. One commandment stands above all others: "Thou shalt love the Lord thy God with all thy heart, and with all thy soul, and with all thy mind. This is the first and great commandment" (Matt. 22:37–38). The great miracle of God's love is that it works in two distinct ways: we receive it, and then we reciprocate it. The Prophet Joseph taught, "A man filled with the love of God, is not content with blessing his family alone, but ranges through the whole world, anxious to bless the whole human race" (*History of the Church* 4:227).

If we love God, we will keep His commandments. As we come to truly know God, not only will our hearts change, but every aspect of our lives will change—our actions, our motives, our words. Even our thoughts. We will truly become new creatures.

The Miracle of His Mighty Love

I got my list about Heavenly Father ready to give to my friend Angela—but before I did, I embarked on a hike to the top of a mountain. I'm not a fast hiker, but I was a determined hiker. My purpose was simple and ancient: I wanted to commune with God. Your process for communing with Him might be very different from mine, but I believe our experiences would have much in common. For that reason, I'd like to share mine.

It took a long time and a great deal of effort to make it to the top of the mountain. I didn't wait to get to the top before I started praying. I prayed with every step I took. Mostly, my prayer was wordless. I listened more than I talked, which is unusual for me, but doing so led to one of the most spiritual experiences of all.

Along the way I saw a great variety of trees and plants. I saw colorful rocks and boulders the size of automobiles. I breathed air that was fresh and fragrant. Above me stretched a sky that changed from blue to gray and back to blue again. Birds filled the air with music, each one singing its own song. Two rabbits chased each other across the path in front of me. Quail scampered everywhere. Deer broke through the underbrush. White and gold butterflies fluttered in the sunlight.

Alma was so right: All things denote there is a God—even the earth, and all things that are on it (see Alma 30:44). Paul, too, was right: "We are the offspring of God" (Acts 17:29). As such, we are one of those creations—one of His creations.

All those years I thought I knew God, I barely even knew *about* Him. Now that my relationship with Him was growing, I thought of my own six children. My heart was so full of love for them, it nearly exploded. Do they always please me? No, they don't. Sometimes they do exactly the opposite of what pleases me. But do I stop loving them because of their behavior? Not for a second.

Why had I been so convinced that I was a disappointment to God and not worthy of His love? When I know that my child is doing his very best against difficult circumstances, I love him that much more.

Finally, I was beginning to get it.

How to Know Him

If we are going to survive when we hit hard places in the road of life, we have to know who God is and who we are in relation to Him. Since Jesus knows the Father best, I paused there in the fading sunshine and read one of the most revealing accounts of God the Father that there is, in the words of his eldest Son: "If a son shall ask bread of any of you that is a father, will he give him a stone? or if he ask a fish, will he for a fish give him a serpent? Or if he shall ask an egg, will he offer him a scorpion? If ye then, being evil, know how to give good gifts unto your children: how much more shall your heavenly Father give the Holy Spirit to them that ask him?" (Luke 11:11–13).

I hope those words help you feel in your own heart the unbounded love your Father has for you.

THE DEFINING WORD

On my hike I realized once and for all that it didn't much matter what others thought or said about me. Those things still hurt; my heart is still way too tender. But now I know that what matters is what *God* says. He says I am His offspring. His child. He says my worth is great. He says that He can take what's weak and make it strong. I believe Him!

When I finally made it to the mountain peak, I looked out; in every direction I saw endless beauty and majesty. I saw proof of an Almighty Creator and Artist. I thought of a Primary Sunbeam with his arms stretched wide, and my heart soared. I thought of a prison inmate behind bars and my heart broke, because I wanted her to feel the freedom that I was feeling.

As I was pondering how to present my information to Angela, I glanced down at a tiny rain puddle, blue from the sky's reflection. In it I saw an image of my own face. In that instant I knew without doubt that of all the creations around me—tiny yellow-winged birds, mighty snow-capped mountains, the endless expanse of sky—of all these, I was the greatest creation of the Great Creator. In spite of all my sins, mistakes, and flaws, I was loved beyond bounds. It is the same for Angela . . . for every one of us.

In that sacred chapel, a church without walls, I fell to my knees and uttered a wordless prayer of gratitude. And now I beg you to do the same.

Study all you can about the Great Parent of the universe. Try with all your heart to keep His commandments. Repent when you don't. Spend time with Him. Serve Him.

Most of all, plead that through the Holy Spirit, you might understand your true identity and infinite worth. For above all that

God has done, He has created you. And above everything that God is, He is your Father.

TRUTH #2:
Jesus Is Our Savior

Rejoice in Christ Jesus, and have no confidence in the flesh.
—Philippians 3:3

I was once invited to speak to a congregation in the deep South. Apparently they didn't know I was LDS until I arrived, because the minister seemed utterly shocked when he said some negative things about Latter-day Saints and I told him I was one. His hospitality suddenly turned into hostility. When he introduced me, he said with no hidden disdain that the Mormon Church "is a Christian-like church."

I was tempted to correct him but sensed that the best doctrine I could possibly teach would come not through my words, but my actions. The next few hours I was on my best behavior, because I felt like I was truly representing Jesus Christ.

After I finished speaking, a number of people approached me and said something to the effect of, "Well, you sure could pass for a real Christian."

I don't know if the words were meant as a compliment, but that's how I chose to interpret them. I smiled, grateful for the spiritual help I'd received in fighting the feelings of the flesh. I did my best to convey the fact that my faith—all of it—hinges on my belief in Jesus Christ and my devotion to His gospel.

When we embraced at my departure, the minister whispered in my ear, "We have nothing in common, Christians and Mormons."

My eyebrows arched as I backed up. "Is Jesus your Savior?" I asked.

"Yes, ma'am!" he said in his rich Southern drawl.

"He's my Savior too."

The smirk melted from the man's face, and I had to fight the one that threatened to break out on mine.

That is the essence of my belief: Jesus Christ is my Savior. It's that simple. It's that wonderful.

Why, then, have I spent so much of my life feeling unworthy to be saved?

REMINDERS

How in the world did I lose my way into such darkness when I was trying so hard to follow the Master? One of the most profound messages Elder Neal A. Maxwell ever delivered was entitled, "Notwithstanding My Weakness." It addressed people like me, like you—people who feel a sense of personal inadequacy in spite of our best efforts. He spoke to those who, despite valiant efforts, continually feel they are forever falling short (see *Ensign,* Nov. 1976, 12).

He was describing me. I had listened to the great enemy, to the judgments of other people, and to the negative voice that came out of my own mouth—but I had somehow silenced the voice that matters most: the voice of my Lord. I had silenced the voice that spoke of my own worth.

I needed reminding. I needed to remember that Jesus Christ is my Savior—which means He deems me worth saving. I needed to remember that He loves me more than I love myself.

I, and all of us, need to understand a pivotal truth: it is that loving Lord who must define us, not the harsh voices inside our own heads—and not any other "voice" that threatens to make us less.

One of the most frequent questions posed to the Prophet Joseph Smith concerned the heart of religion. His answer was the guide that gave me direction in my quest to listen to the right voice: "The fundamental principles of our religion are the testimony of the Apostles and Prophets, concerning Jesus Christ, that He died, was buried, and rose again the third day, and ascended into heaven; and all other things which pertain to our religion are only appendages to it" (Joseph Fielding Smith, *Teachings of the Prophet Joseph Smith* [Salt Lake City: Deseret Book Company, 1976], 121).

Jesus is the heart and soul of our faith. As such, the ultimate voice belongs to Him. Why, then, do we put so much stock in what others think of us—even, or maybe *especially*, what we think of ourselves?

What think ye of Christ? I've come to realize that the answer to that question defines my life. If I really believe that Christ is the Son of God, my personal Savior, a Lord of love and mercy, then everything changes—because Christ defines me as God's child, an individual of inestimable worth, someone worthy of the infinite sacrifice. He feels the same about you . . . about all of us.

As we come to know our Savior, we will come to know ourselves.

SPIRITUAL IDENTITY

The world defines us in many ways: by our bank account, the size of our house, the age and shine of our automobiles, the label of our clothing, and the number on our scale. I bought into all of that—and then spent years berating myself, agreeing with those who said I was worthless and unworthy and incapable.

They were wrong, and so was I. The devil told me that degrading myself demonstrated humility. I wasn't being humble; I was being stupid. I was doing the devil's work *for* him by tearing myself down.

All of that stopped when I began to understand my spiritual identity as *Christ* defined it. Imagine the impact we would have on the world if we, as God's covenant people, moved through every day with the power and purpose and grace that Christ knows we have!

How does it work? In order to know ourselves, we must first come to know God the Father. There is only one way to do that— through our Redeemer, Jesus Christ, who said, "I am the way, the truth, and the life: no man cometh unto the Father, but by me" (John 14:6). It is critical, then, that we also come to know the Savior.

There are many ways to come to know the Savior. Your journey will be unique to your circumstances, just as mine was to my circumstances. But I believe your journey and mine will have some things in common. In my life, four things led to a closer walk with Jesus: finding facts, mustering faith, following in His footsteps, and using the force of Jesus Christ.

FINDING FACTS

It is paramount that we remember the exchange between Jesus and Peter when they were discussing the Savior's true identity. Jesus looked into the eyes of His disciple and asked, "But whom say ye that I am?"

Remember Peter's answer? "And Simon Peter answered and said, Thou art the Christ, the Son of the living God. And Jesus answered and said unto him, Blessed art thou, Simon Bar-jona: for flesh and blood hath not revealed it unto thee, but my Father which is in heaven" (Matt. 16:15–18).

Therein is the key. We can assemble facts about Jesus until the day He comes again. We can read stacks of books. We can watch every movie ever made about Christ. But until and unless the Holy Ghost bears witness to us that Jesus is our Savior, all we have is "head knowledge." We need "heart knowledge"—the kind that comes from Heavenly Father, the kind that is embossed in our souls through the witness of the Holy Spirit, the kind that seals our hearts to the Savior. Once we have that kind of knowledge— once our spirits *know* who Jesus really is—no voice on earth can make us doubt.

With that important reminder, facts are a great way to lay the foundation for a relationship. "Facts" seem to be a rather clinical way of getting to know someone—but unless you have the facts, it's easy to be deceived or misled. People have tried to tell me that Jesus was simply a very good man—maybe even a prophet—but certainly not the Son of God. The facts speak otherwise.

As you examine the facts, consider how Jesus defined Himself. With divine humility, He declared: "I am the light and the life of the world. I am Alpha and Omega, the beginning and the end" (3 Ne. 9:18). He declared that He was "Jesus Christ, your Redeemer, the Great I Am" (D&C 29:1).

A college professor once assigned me to write a paper on an influential man named Johannes Chrysostomus Wolfgangus Theophilus Mozart. The great composer had been dead for centuries, yet his music lived on—proof that he had indeed existed. I started by getting the basic facts in order: he was born in 1756 in Salzburg, Austria. His father later shortened

Wolfgangus to *Wolfgang,* and adopted *Amadeus,* the Latin version of "Theophilus."

Young Mozart learned to love music as a result of studying with his father, a composer and violinist. By the age of six Mozart was composing and performing music in public. Much of his life was spent traveling. His career met with many ups and downs; his financial standing was never secure, and his popularity also fluctuated. The brilliance of his talent was not fully appreciated until long after he was dead.

Mozart lived slightly more than 13,000 days on earth, devoted to his passion for music. He fell in love and suffered the pain of romantic rejection. Years later he married the sister of the woman who had declined him. Only two of their six children survived beyond infancy. When Mozart died at age thirty-five from an undetermined medical condition, he was buried without fanfare in an unmarked pauper's grave in Vienna.

I learned a lot of facts about Mozart, but I didn't really come to know him until I sat at the piano and worked tirelessly to make my fingers follow the black and white notes that led me down the same pathways Mozart had marked. Only then did he become real to me.

Years later, when I was desperately praying for guidance, the Holy Ghost assigned me a different topic: Jesus Christ. The Spirit had whispered, "Take your eyes off yourself and focus on my Son." I wanted to be obedient. If I really was a Christian, worthy to bear Christ's name, it meant I had to believe, even though all I had were shards of shattered faith. In spite of my circumstances, God had a better plan for my life. He is the Great Restorer. He had a brighter day waiting.

The only way I could reclaim my life was to increase my faith in Jesus.

I tried, but staying focused on Christ was not so easy. As one problem in my life got solved, another bigger one would emerge. It seemed a lot like that amusement park game where monster heads pop up: you hit one with a hammer, and two more appear. Maybe you've had times in your life like that. I was focused on everything that was wrong in my life while God was trying to get me to focus on all that was right—and Jesus defines righteousness.

Finally I started to get it, and my simple prayer went something like this: "Oh Father, I'm a mess. My life is a mess. I make no excuses. I place blame on no one but myself. I can't do this alone; I don't *want* to do it alone. Please help me replace the fear with faith. Lead every step I take. Show me how to forgive—to forget myself and focus on Jesus."

At first I felt like nothing changed.

But through the blur of tears I read scriptures that seemed to reinforce what the Holy Ghost had whispered: "feast upon the words of Christ; for behold, the words of Christ will tell you all things what ye should do" (2 Ne. 32:3). And the Savior's own words said it best: "Look unto me in every thought; doubt not, fear not" (D&C 6:36).

Faith cannot exist where fear thrives, so it was time for me to step up to a higher level of discipleship. No more lukewarm living. It was time to go from good to better, from better to best, because anything less than my best simply was not enough to call down the powers of heaven that I needed.

What a dilemma: the Spirit was demanding the best of me when I was at my very worst. Just as when I was seeking to know God the Father, I knew I needed an increase in faith. True discipleship means true discipline—and it was time to shape up. I needed to curb my tongue from speaking anything—anything at all—that wasn't positive and true.

I had to start saying positive things about myself or I simply had to shut up. Both choices proved to be a true challenge, but it was a challenge issued by Jesus himself: "But those things which proceed out of the mouth come forth from the heart; and they defile the man" (Matt. 15:18).

I quickly learned that becoming a true disciple had very little to do with what was going on outside of me, and everything to do with what was going on *inside* of me. It was time to change from the inside out—beginning with my thoughts, my words, my actions.

I had a lot of repenting to do.

I had a lot of work to do.

I *thought* I had a testimony before. All my years of Church service, scripture study, teaching, and striving had blessed me with a testimony. But a *testimony* of Jesus Christ is not the same as having a *relationship* with our Savior. Just like I prayed to the Father to better know the Father, I prayed to the Father to better know His Son. I ached to have a true and abiding relationship with my Redeemer, to know without doubt that I was finally focusing where I needed to focus.

Here's the real deal: I had believed the wrong voices because I had not paid enough attention to the voice that should rise above all other voices. I had been a casual Christian, a mediocre Mormon. I had been at a stalemate for too long. It was time to take a flying leap of faith.

I prayed harder than ever to know my Savior and to feel His strength seep into my soul; I used everything I'd learned about God the Father and begged to better know my Savior. But when

I got up from my knees and looked around, everything appeared the same. Everything felt the same.

My heart was drawn back to the story of a young farm boy, David O. McKay, whose father was serving a mission in Scotland. Young David felt a tremendous responsibility to help care for his family and to know for himself that what Joseph Smith said happened had *really* happened. He wanted nothing more than a revelation about the reality of God the Father and Jesus Christ.

Just outside of Huntsville, Utah, not far from the family farm, David rode his horse to a secluded area to do exactly what Joseph had done—to pray for truth and revelation. He had high expectations; in describing the experience, he says that he knelt beneath a serviceberry bush and prayed that God would "declare to him the truth of his revelation to Joseph Smith" (in Leon Hartshorn, "David O. McKay: The Worth of a Soul," *New Era,* Jan. 1972, 56). Young David's prayer was heartfelt. He prayed with as much faith as he could muster. After saying "Amen," he waited. But there was no voice from heaven. No angel. Nothing, it seemed, had changed. A disappointed David climbed back on his horse and rode away slowly, saying to himself, "No spiritual manifestation has come to me. If I am true to myself, I must say I am just the same 'old boy' that I was before I prayed."

That's exactly how I felt: I was the same "old girl" as I had been before I prayed. The pain had not vanished. Fear still clutched my throat. But I was desperate to obey—so I went on praying, even when a voice inside my head told me that my prayers were foolish and unfruitful because *I* was foolish and unfruitful.

I prayed for those thoughts of unworthiness to be silenced. I tried to make my supplications new and challenging. No matter how I framed it, one request was consistent: I prayed to the Father to better know the Son.

When nothing appeared to happen, I decided to act in desperate faith. Again, your individual journey may be much different from mine, but I want to describe the path I took, because I am confident our journeys will have many principles in common. I wanted to know about the Savior, so I turned to technology I had consulted before when I found myself wanting knowledge: I turned on my computer and did a search for *Jesus Christ*. That search yielded 43 million results.

Right away, I found that He lived on earth approximately one thousand days fewer than Mozart had lived. I decided to compile a complete biography about the greatest man who ever lived, much the same as I had done about the great composer. I borrowed stacks of books from the library. I invested in a new set of scriptures and marked every quote that fell from the lips of Jesus. I found historical dates. I studied pictures of landmarks that dated to ancient Palestine. I read about the circumstances of Christ's birth, His family background, the political and historical climate of the Holy Land. I discovered how Jewish boys were educated in that day. I researched the lineage of David and other branches of Christ's early family.

I filled notebooks with information.

I even wrote a novel incorporating the information I learned.

Ever so gradually, my scripture study began to yield a change within me. I was not only learning about Christ, I was learning who I am in and through Him. As one scholar so aptly described it, "In the scriptures man finds that he belongs to a whole, of which God is a part. . . . A devout use of the scriptures nourishes the spiritual life with a calm that displaces the doubts and anxieties which paralyze mankind" (George T. Boyd, *Views on Man and Religion,* in Victor L. Brown, "Finding One's Identity," *Ensign,* May 1983, 60).

GETTING THE FACTS STRAIGHT

Using the scriptures, I made lists of facts about the Savior. I'd like to suggest that you sit down with your scriptures and make your own list. It's a great launching pad.

To sum things up, here is what I learned. Jesus is the Beloved, Only Begotten Son of God. He dwelt in the same heavens where we dwelt as spirit children of the Father. Jesus is central to our Father's plan—a plan that sent us to earth to be tested for a probationary period, during which time we would experience joy and sorrow and everything in between. That plan would let us prove ourselves through the principle of free agency (see Moses 4:1–4).

As part of that plan, Jesus volunteered to give His life that we might live. He was willingly obedient. We often talk about the love the Father has for the Son, but don't often focus on the love the Son has for the Father. When the Father's plan of salvation and happiness was presented (see Alma 34:9; 42:5, 8), one was required to provide redemption and mercy to atone for all those who accepted the plan (see Alma 34:16; 39:18; 42:15). The eldest, the most worthy, volunteered, "Father, thy will be done, and the glory be thine forever" (Moses 4:2). "The Father sent the Son to be the Saviour of the world" (1 Jn. 4:14).

Jesus is the second member of the Godhead. He is *like* the Father, a glorified being of power and authority, but is an individual. Jesus Christ is a god; He is the Jehovah of the Old Testament and the Savior of the New Testament (see Abr. 2:7–8).

Under the direction of the Father, Jesus created this earth and countless others: "And worlds without number have I created; and I also created them for mine own purpose; and by the Son I created them, which is mine Only Begotten" (Moses 1:33). "There is none other name under heaven given among men, whereby we must be saved" (Acts 4:12).

Jesus exemplifies the Father. In fact, Jesus let Himself be defined not by the world, but by His Father. He testified during His great intercessory prayer, "O righteous Father, the world hath not known thee: but I have known thee, and [the Apostles] have known that thou hast sent me" (John 17:25). What a great lesson for me to learn!

Jesus does not change; He is the same yesterday, and today, and forever (see Heb. 13:8). Jesus is all powerful (see Matt. 28:18). Jesus is all knowing (see Col. 2:3). Jesus is our Mediator with the Father, and as such, He pleads our cause with the Father (see D&C 76:41–43; John 3:17)

As the Savior of humanity, Jesus is the ultimate humanitarian. Through Him and by Him shall all mankind be saved.

Jesus understands. Because He descended below all things (see D&C 122:8), He knows how to lift us above our daily difficulties. He came to earth to gain experience, and He gained it by living life to a fullness few of us can comprehend. We can never say that Jesus doesn't understand what we are feeling or thinking or doing, because He does understand, completely and empathetically.

Jesus is gentle and forgiving. Remember that Joseph Smith had confidence to go into that grove to pray because James had promised that we can ask of God without fearing reproach (see James 1:5). He knows that we make mistakes—big, dumb mistakes—yet He never condemns us. His spirit will convict us to turn us to repentance, but Jesus will never beat us up with guilt or condemnation. He understands because He made Himself like us (see Heb. 2:17)

Jesus lived for us. Jesus extended to us the invitation, "Come, follow me," that we might know what it is like to live in peace and freedom from sin—in joy along the journey. And Jesus died for us so we might come unto Him: "For, behold, the Lord your Redeemer suffered death in the flesh; wherefore he suffered the pain of all men, that all men might repent and come unto him" (D&C 18:11). He *begs* us to take advantage of His atonement.

Jesus defeated death (see 1 Cor. 15:4). Jesus showed Himself to those He loved and those who believed in Him (see John 10:11). Jesus ascended to heaven before the eyes of His disciples with the promise that He would come again in like manner (see Luke 24:51–53; Acts 1:9–11).

Jesus has made Himself known in these latter days and will again make Himself known in the last days (see D&C 102:9). Jesus Christ leads and guides His Church today through revelation to a prophet.

Facts are important, because they are the beginning of understanding. But facts mean nothing until they are put to the test by faith.

MUSTERING FAITH

I don't know about you, but I had to believe that Jesus understood everything about me. I had to believe He knew my heart, even the shadowy places that I didn't know myself. I had to believe that He understood my past, my weaknesses, and my strengths. I had to believe what it seemed impossible to believe—that He was on my side, that He wanted me to be happy and confident and at peace.

I had to believe it even when I didn't *feel* it, because I believed that His mission is to save me from my sins and from myself.

I need to make something clear: faith is not a *feeling;* it's much, much more than that. If we wait to be motivated by feelings, we're in for a long wait. How many times have you said or heard someone else say, "I just don't *feel* like it"? If we wait around to *feel* like doing good, we're in trouble. I'll be honest: I didn't *feel* like getting up in the mornings. I didn't *feel* like saying my prayers. I didn't *feel* like reading my scriptures. I didn't even *feel* like going to church—but, then, I don't suppose Jesus much *felt* like going to the cross. Yet we do what we do out of faith—and faith is a decision to go forward, to do what's right, no matter how we feel.

Remember the boyhood prayer of David O. McKay? He was a grown man before that prayer was answered. While serving a mission in Scotland, Elder McKay received a powerful spiritual manifestation—an assurance and emotion like he had never felt. He knew it was the answer he had prayed so earnestly for as a young boy beneath that serviceberry bush (see Francis M. Gibbons, *David O. McKay* [Salt Lake City: Deseret Book Co., 1986], 50). That assurance applied to me too, just as it applies to all of us. For me, change didn't come immediately, and it didn't arrive wrapped as a miracle. But as I persisted in faith, I began to feel a change taking place deep inside—a new breaking of my heart. And though I knew my efforts were inadequate, they were accepted. Mahatma Gandhi taught that whatever you do will be inadequate, but it is paramount that you do it.

Oh, the devil doesn't like it when we forget ourselves and remember Jesus. Every day I had to fight through the obstacles Satan put in my way. My thoughts had to stay focused on Jesus and His mercy. I had to change, and so did my words. I could no longer say, "My life is a mess." Instead, I had to say, "The Lord is going to take my mess and make it His message. Wait and see." I memorized scriptures that gave me hope. I spoke them aloud when I was alone.

In the midst of my greatest pain, I found simple little ways to serve others, and at those times, I discovered that I was really serving myself. I accepted invitations to speak. I bore fervent testimony of the Lord's power to save—even though I didn't yet feel saved. There were times I was so sad and so weak I didn't think that I could do it, but with His help I smiled though my tears and I promised the Lord that I would not wait until the end of my trial to praise Him. I promised I would stand as a witness, in the midst of the storm, and proclaim that I knew He had the power to calm the seas—and that He *would* calm the seas when He decided the storm had accomplished its purpose.

FOLLOWING IN HIS FOOTSTEPS

I was learning to *say* the right things, but what is talk without action? We follow Christ when we become more like Him—when we obey His commandments and then witness for ourselves the blessings that occur as a result (see Dieter F. Uchtdorf, "Developing Christlike Attributes," *Ensign,* Oct. 2008, 5–8). As the facts I had learned about Jesus became intertwined with the faith I was developing, I realized it was time to answer Jesus' bid to follow Him.

If my life was going to get straightened out, I had to get up and move forward with a sense of purpose and hope. I had to step through the darkness and into the light, forward in a way that was foreign to me. I went back to the scriptures and studied not only what Jesus said, but what He did. He served. He loved. He worked. He rested. He prayed with fervor. He was patient and kind—mild, yet strong. He never once put Himself down or allowed others to determine His course.

I realized that if I was going to be defined by Christ, I could not allow anyone to push me around and down again. Not anyone.

It occurred to me that I would benefit from talking about the Savior with people I believed really knew Jesus on an intimate, powerful level. How had they developed such strong faith in their relationship with Christ? I made a very personal, private list of people whose lives I believed emulated the Savior's. I made appointments. I tucked my scriptures beneath my arm, bought a new notebook and more red pencils, and then went from example to example to learn what I could.

The first thing I discovered is that every single one of the people I'd deemed most Christlike had weathered great adversity. *Every single one of them.* As Elder Neal A. Maxwell observed, if our souls were marked by rings, as are trees, the years of greatest personal growth would likely be those characterized by the greatest moisture—not as the result of rainfall, but of tears (see Neal A. Maxwell, "Thanks Be to God," *Ensign,* Jul. 1982, 51). I learned, too, that not one of these most acquainted with the Savior would trade his trials for the faith he had built or the relationship she had fortified with Jesus.

The second thing members of this group had in common was valor. They served with their whole beings to build the kingdom of God. They did not neglect prayer or scripture study. The temple was a holy place for them, and they made time to be there regularly. They accepted whatever callings came to them and tried their best to magnify their responsibilities. They came early and stayed late. They cleaned up messes made by others. They were willing to pay the price of unseen service. They served with valor when no one but God could see them serving.

My examples varied. They came from different places, races, and stations in life. There were men and women, young and aged. Some had large homes; some simply rented apartments.

But there was much they had in common. They shared peace—a happiness and joy in their countenances. They were kind and gentle. They all laughed, especially at their own expense, but not one of them said or did anything to injure his or her own soul or diminish his or her value.

I noticed that they were not busy people, but they were fruitful people. They invested their resources rather than spending them. They loved their families and friends and managed to keep priorities in place. They'd done time in the trenches serving the less fortunate. They kept the commandments—not perfectly, but consistently. They had been humbled through repentance. They understood that the power of the Atonement was not just to cover sin, but to soothe suffering.

One man told me that following Jesus was never meant to be a part-time hobby, but a full-time commitment. One woman told me that she saw the image of Jesus reflected in the eyes of every person she saw. Another shared how the examples of others had introduced her to the Savior: "We come to know Him as we come to know those who know Him."

I heard all kinds of experiences from all kinds of people. I learned that every journey to meet the Savior is different, but that every such journey includes obedience and desire.

I went back to my own life. I returned to my writings, my diaries, my journals. I revisited my memories—the deepest ones—asking that the Holy Ghost bring to my remembrance the times that Jesus had extended mercy to me, times when Christ's strength had become my strength, times when His wisdom had provided the answers I needed.

Something remarkable happened as a result. I came to a profound realization: all those years that I had tried so hard but had failed had not been wasted. I found that Jesus wasn't as unfamiliar to me as I had thought.

I realized that Jesus had always been there for me. If you will look back with spiritual scrutiny—if you will take the time and invest the effort to make a record—you will see too that He has never left you. That's not all: He will never leave you.

Using the Force of Jesus Christ

All the work I'd done felt somehow preparatory. If I really wanted my life to change from the inside out, if I really wanted to silence the Pharisees, I needed great force. I needed to know more than the fact that Jesus atoned for me: I needed to know how to apply that Atonement, that power, that all-encompassing force in my life.

Did that mean that something significant had to happen? Did I need to see a vision or hear a voice? No. The Atonement works just like the Spirit—it comes in small increments and in whispered assurances. Elijah's understanding of this principle is clear: "And he said, Go forth, and stand upon the mount before the Lord. And, behold, the Lord passed by, and a great and strong wind rent the mountains, and brake in pieces the rocks before the Lord; but the Lord was not in the wind: and after the wind an earthquake; but the Lord was not in the earthquake: And after the earthquake a fire; but the Lord was not in the fire: and after the fire a still small voice" (1 Kgs. 19:11–13).

That still, small voice never whispers, "You're not worthy. You have no value. You can't do it."

That still, small voice whispers, "Come unto me."

Come means we have to approach Him. To *come* requires initiative and effort on our part. He's there waiting with arms open. He was there yesterday. He'll be there tomorrow. We're the ones who have to move.

No human mind can fully grasp the gift of Christ's atonement, the vastness and inclusiveness of the act—but in the end, it comes down to just you and Jesus. You've come, and He's met you with open arms—and now it's just between the two of you. As C. S. Lewis wrote, "[God] has infinite attention to spare for each one of us. He does not have to deal with us in the mass. You are as much alone with Him as if you were the only being He had ever created. When Christ died, He died for you individually just as much as if you had been the only man [or woman] in the world" (*Mere Christianity* [1943], 131).

Slowly—and oh, so painfully—I began what President Thomas S. Monson describes as a transformation (see "My Personal Hall of Fame," *Ensign,* Jul. 1991, 2). Throughout that process, even when I could not articulate the depth of my emotions, I knew Jesus understood. "For we have not an high priest which cannot be touched with the feelings of our infirmities, but was in all points tempted like as we are, yet without sin. Let us therefore come boldly unto the throne of grace, that we may obtain mercy, and find grace to help in time of need" (Heb. 4:15–16).

Confidence in Christ

I realized I'd never had confidence—not real, lasting confidence—because I had never put my confidence in the Worthy One. That began to change as I began to trust in Christ and in His love and in the redeeming, restoring power of His Atonement.

Confidence was cultivated as I realized that Jesus is Savior to *all* of us—those who suffer hurt as well as those who inflict it. I've done my share of both.

My confidence waxed strong when I realized *why* Christ did what He did in suffering and atoning for *my* sins: "For, behold, the Lord your Redeemer suffered death in the flesh; wherefore he suffered the pain of all men, that all men might repent and come unto him" (D&C 18:11). Jesus suffered and atoned so that I could come to Him, so that I would cry on His shoulder during those unending nights of darkness, so that I could lay my heartbreaking burden at His feet.

He overcame so that I could come to Him.

I beg you to do the same.

Come to Christ. Know Him. Trust Him. Follow Him. "Believe in God; believe that he is, and that he created all things, both in heaven and in earth; believe that he has all wisdom, and all power, both in heaven and in earth; believe that man doth not comprehend all the things which the Lord can comprehend. . . . Believe that ye must repent of your sins and forsake them, and humble yourselves before God; and ask in sincerity of heart that he would forgive you; and now, if you believe all these things see that ye do them" (Mosiah 4:9–10).

Don't just come to Him when you're in pain and suffering. Show up at the throne of grace when your day is filled with sunshine and your heart is pounding with gratitude. Those days are important too, because every day, every pain, every experience that we incur in life is important in helping us become the strong, confident, faith-filled people we are meant to become.

There are no words to describe the power of the Atonement and what it has come to mean in my life. We have the right to lay claim on it. But that's not all: As members of His Church, we have a *responsibility* to lay claim on that power.

As I have refocused my thoughts, my words, and my deeds on Jesus and no one else, my life has seen mighty change. You too can change your life; you can have and enjoy the life that Jesus atoned for you to have, if you will focus on Him.

Discover all you can about your Savior. Test His word. Allow Him to carry the burdens that buckle your knees. Have faith in what He says—so much faith that you go out and do what He did. Use the force of Christ's Atonement.

It works.

I promise—it works.

TRUTH #3:
Our Worth Is Infinite

There is therefore now no condemnation
to them which are in Christ Jesus.
—Romans 8:1

Years ago I was anxious as I prepared to make a presentation to the largest group of people I'd ever spoken to. I went before the Lord and asked for inspiration on what I should say.

Tell them that I love them, the Spirit whispered.

Sure, I'll do that, but what should my topic be? I want something unique and truly inspirational.

Tell them that I love them.

I will, but what I need is a focal point, a hook that they will remember.

Tell them that I love them.

It took a while, but I finally understood—the most important message of all lies in knowing that we are loved by our Father in Heaven and by His Son, our Savior. There is no more powerful headline, no greater news to broadcast. Every message I've taught since then has had the same focus: God loves you! If there is one thing I know I'm on this earth to do, it's to shout that truth from the rooftops.

Sometimes it's easy for us to tell others they are loved, but not so easy to believe it of ourselves—not because we don't think God loves His children, but because we may feel undeserving of His love. The adversary loves to remind us who we are not. Not pretty. Not smart. Not strong.

And his destructive voice might not be the only voice we hear. Satan is skilled at recruiting other people to reinforce his cruelties and his lies. Some of the people he uses to convey his message are those who supposedly care most about us—and they are the ones who inflict the deepest wounds. I wonder how often we say unkind words to people without realizing the damage we are doing to their spirits. I wonder how often our tongues are on the errand of evil without even realizing it.

Mark Twain advised, "Keep away from small people who try to belittle your ambitions. Small people always do that, but the really great make you feel that you, too, can become great."

Jesus teaches us that we can be great—great like Him: "If any man serve me, let him follow me" (John 12:26).

The most destructive thing we can possibly do in life is to make another person doubt his worth and identity as a child of God. The very most productive thing we can do is to help ourselves and others realize that as children of God, our worth is infinite.

A Simple Miracle

One night in the Tel Aviv airport I was witness to a sort of simple miracle, if there are such things as simple miracles. A slight-framed, elderly man was resting on a chair near our boarding gate. His eyes were closed and his head back. When the flight was called, he seemed startled and jumped up, leaving his black bag of belongings beneath his seat as he hurried to step into line.

My friend saw what he'd done and raced to tell him. In the meantime, I waited by his seat to protect his belongings.

"Sir, is that your bag beneath the chair?" my friend called.

At first the man seemed offended. He looked at her with a harsh frown. When he realized his mistake, his frown vanished. A look of intense emotion twisted his lined face. Tears sprang from his eyes and he came back over to where I was, reached beneath his seat, cradled his bag, and then collapsed beside me in his chair.

"Are you all right?" I whispered.

His whole body shook. "Do you know what would have happened to me if I'd lost this? Do you know what would have happened?" His palm slapped his forehead, and his voice rose so loud that people around us stopped to stare. "My life would be ruined if I lost this bag."

By now my friend had walked away to stand in line, and I was alone, kneeling beside the man. "Sir, but you didn't lose your bag. It's with you," I said, smiling, trying to assure him. "It just proves that God loves you."

The man stiffened. His dark eyes went to slits. "What did you say?"

"I said your bag is safe. No one took it or even touched it."

"No. No. What did you say about God?"

"I said He's watching over you, protecting you because He loves you."

The hard lines in his face deepened. He sat up and clutched his bag tight to his chest, so tight the color from his knuckles drained. "How dare you say that to me."

"Because it's true. God loves you."

The man struggled to stand up. His whole body was racked with emotion. There was a sudden curve to his upper lip as he spit the words back at me. "God doesn't love me. He never has. I am a child of World War II Europe. God has never loved me!"

By now my friend was waving me over to join her at the boarding gate. By now our little conversation was garnering more attention than I wanted. I simply smiled. "We'd better hurry; they are calling for us to board."

With a wave of his hand, he brushed me off. "I'll come along. You go."

I was already in my seat when the man filed past while boarding the plane. He stopped and raised his chin, still shaking, when he saw me. "What you said back there—I wish I believed it, but it's not true."

"Oh, but it is, sir. It's always been true, always will be true."

"You don't know what I've been through."

"No, I don't. But God does."

"I don't believe it."

"That's okay," I told him. "I believe it enough for both of us."

The hardness in his eyes seemed to soften. He didn't exactly smile, but his frown was gone.

Once the plane was in the air and all had become dark and quiet, I got up to use the restroom. The old man appeared to be asleep in an aisle seat, and as I walked past him, I said a silent prayer, imagining the horrors that he'd survived, the sadness of believing that God had withheld His love. On the way back to my own seat, the man's hand reached out and stopped me. He motioned for me to kneel beside him. He whispered, "Are you sure?"

"Yes, I'm sure."

His chin quivered. His cheeks were wet. "Absolutely sure?"

"Absolutely, sir. God loves you."

For a quiet time I just knelt there beside him, my hand atop his, while he wept. There was nothing more that I could say. The Spirit would have to bear witness to him if he were to feel the truth. When the moment was over, he briskly brushed me away again, and I went back to my seat with tears on my own cheeks.

I didn't see him again until we were caught in the crowd of disembarking passengers. It was morning, and there was a smile on his face. No, it was a grin. He wore a wide grin, and he made sure our eyes met. Clutching his black bag with one arm, he lifted the other to wave at me, but then he pressed two fingers to his lips and blew me a kiss.

A simple miracle?

I don't think so. I don't think there are such things as *simple* miracles.

Imagine how the world would change if every person felt that divine connection—a spiritual assurance that we are of infinite worth because we are children of Deity!

With all my heart I pray that your heart can break wide open so that you can feel and receive the assurance that you are loved by God the Father and your Savior, Jesus Christ. There is no more powerful source on earth.

I had not suffered the atrocities that man suffered, but I knew what it felt like to think that God loved others, but could not love me because I was undeserving. It was only through the atoning force of Jesus Christ that a storm began to rise inside of me, to blow away the lies and the debris, to clear away the clouds and let the very source of light finally speak the truth: I belong to God. As His daughter, I have direct access to the Father of the Universe, day or night. Out of that unfathomable love a Savior was sent to save me.

What does Christ think of me? With all my sins and all my flaws, I am deemed deserving of divine love. Christ stands ready to make up for all that I lack. His Atonement doesn't just cover my sins, it consoles my suffering.

There is no lack of suffering in this world. I think of some of the people I know. A woman who lost her husband to divorce and her son to suicide. A man whose wife left him to raise their five children so she could "enjoy life." A woman, who after twenty-six years of an abusive marriage took a revolver and shot her husband. A young man who is confused about his sexuality and feels alienated and alone. A young woman who is in so much pain she slices herself with a razor blade. A friend who battles cancer while trying to raise a houseful of young boys. Another friend who has seen her daughter let go of the iron rod and travel through life without the gospel. A grandmother who has taken in her seven grandchildren even though she is in her seventies. A former bishop who looked over the edge to see what Satan had to offer and who has fallen so low he thinks even the arm of God can't reach him now.

I am affiliated with a children's service foundation through which I travel and see the suffering that children in this world endure. I won't describe it, because I don't have the words. But if you have ever held a dying AIDS baby in your arms, you cannot doubt that angels surround that child. God loves that child and cries the tears his little dehydrated eyes are too dry to cry.

God's love is everywhere there is goodness . . . even, and especially, where there is suffering.

It might not seem like it through the eyes of the world, but we see God with different eyes . . . or at least we should.

Our Idea of God's Love

This is His invitation: "Look unto me in every thought; doubt not, fear not" (D&C 6:36). That scripture spoke to me saying that if I'm looking to the Savior, thinking as He thinks, then there is no room for self-doubt and no space for fear. There is no scale where one person weighs in more valuable than another. Feelings of depression and inadequacy do nothing but destroy—and God's work is about *building,* not destroying.

Why is it that we tend to measure our worst against someone else's best? Doing so makes it difficult to understand the leniency and love with which Jesus judges us. Keeping our focus on the Savior keeps our focus off ourselves. It allows us to be more aware, more grateful, more positive, and even more humble. It allows us to become our strongest, best selves.

Get It Right

I have had the privilege of standing at Caesarea Philippi, where Jesus asked, "Whom say ye that I am?"

Our individual salvation hinges on our response and our subsequent devotion to that answer.

Peter got it right: "Thou art the Christ, the Son of the living God" (Matt. 16:15–16). I'd like to suggest that you change the query. I'm asking you to kneel and pose the question, "Father, Who am I? Who is this person worthy of Christ's salvation?"

The answer will determine the quality of life you will live. If you are not absolutely sure that you are a child of God, then what do you believe about yourself? Believing that you are anything less than a child of Deity is believing less than the truth. All Satan has to do is steal your confidence in this one matter, and he's stolen the quality of your life.

I wish I hadn't wasted so much of my life spiritually confused. I can't change the past, but I can go forward now, living a life defined by Christ. "The Spirit itself beareth witness with our spirit, that we are the children of God" (Rom. 8:16). Nothing less than this truth is acceptable.

Who We Were

To truly understand this reality, let's formulate a foundational definition. Since our spiritual creation, we have been children of the Most High God. There is a part of Him in us, because we are of His divine design and wondrous workmanship. "The Lord said unto Enoch: Behold these thy brethren; they are the workmanship of mine own hands, and I gave unto them their knowledge, in the day I created them; and in the Garden of Eden, gave I unto man his agency" (Moses 7:32).

There are times when I wonder about the premortal existence. What was it like? What was I like there? With whom did I associate? What promises did I make there that must be fulfilled here?

I've had the experience of meeting someone and known without doubt that I was not meeting that person for the first time. It was a reunion of spirits so immediate and intense that it could not be explained or denied. It wasn't like we were getting acquainted; it was like we were being reunited. We knew things about each other without ever explaining. You've probably experienced the same type of thing.

I testify to you that as children of God, we lived before we came here. We learned and loved and laughed together. We were a spiritual family then, and we are a spiritual family now. Elder Marion G. Romney taught, "We were individual, separate persons, with agency, being, and names prior to our entry on earth" (Marion G. Romney, "We Are Children of God," *Ensign,* Sep. 1984, 3).

What were we doing during all that time? Elder Bruce R. McConkie gave this insight: "All the spirits of men, while yet in the Eternal Presence, developed aptitudes, talents, capacities, and abilities of every sort, kind, and degree. During the long expanse of life which then was, an infinite variety of talents and abilities came into being. As the ages rolled, no two spirits remained alike. Mozart became a musician; Einstein centered his interest in mathematics; Michelangelo turned his attention to painting. Cain was a liar, a schemer, a rebel. . . . Mary and Eve were two of the greatest of all the spirit daughters of the Father. . . . And so it went through all the hosts of heaven, each individual developing such talents and abilities as his soul desired" (*The Mortal Messiah: From Bethlehem to Calvary* [Salt Lake City: Deseret Book, 1981], 1:23).

So as you come to understand who you are, you realize that arriving here on earth was not the beginning of life, rather a continuation.

You were entrusted to come to the earth in these last days to do again what you did before—to once again choose good over evil. You have come into the world at a most significant time. We are entering the final stages of a great war. This war commenced before the foundations of the world and has been pursued with awful consequence throughout the world's history. I speak of the war between the followers of Christ and all those who deny Him as their God.

It was Satan who instigated this premortal war. He did so by rebelling against our Father's plan of salvation for His children and rejecting the Christ, who was designated to effectuate the plan. Tragically, a third of our Father's children followed Satan. Yet two-thirds did not. You were among these two-thirds, and with them have come to earth to pursue the Father's plan of happiness.

Unfortunately, Satan's war did not end with his expulsion from heaven. As John observed, Satan and his followers were "cast out into the earth" and have come here with "great wrath" (Rev. 12:9, 12). The evidence of their wrath can be seen in the blood and horror that has afflicted man from the beginning of time.

So profound and extensive have been the wounds suffered among men that God Himself wept as He surveyed man's condition.

While God's kingdom has been established on the earth in times past, the people to whom the kingdom was previously committed were unable to keep it. This time, however, is different. The prophetic promise is that this time God's kingdom will not be lost, but will overcome the world.

To ensure its ultimate success, the final restoration of God's kingdom has been commenced with unprecedented spiritual power and is being sustained by that same spiritual power and something more. Reserved to come forth in these last days and labor for our Father and His Son are some of the most valiant and noble of our Father's sons and daughters. Their valiance and nobility were demonstrated in the pre-earth struggle with Satan. There, "being left to choose good or evil," they "[chose] good" and exhibited "exceedingly great faith" and "good works" (Alma 13:3).

Such are the traits that are now needed to sustain the work of God in the earth and to save the souls of men from the intensifying wrath of the adversary. You are the strength of the Lord's house, those who chose good over evil and who exhibited "exceedingly great faith" and "good works." And because of what you did there, you were entrusted to come to the earth in these last days to do again what you did before—to once again choose good over evil, exercise exceedingly great faith, and perform good works.

You were there. I was there.

We stood for Jesus then, and we must stand for Him still.

Who We Are Now

Our Heavenly Father works with a plan. I've learned that I accomplish much more when I try to operate within that plan. We are sons and daughters of God, here on earth to gain bodies, experiences, and wisdom that we might make a mighty step in becoming like our Father in Heaven. None of us is here without a labor to perform.

Then what gives us our spiritual identity?

Outwardly, I look nothing like my mother. She was petite and had a dark complexion. She was graceful. I resemble my father, who was broad and Scandinavian. He was not so graceful. But inwardly, I have traits from each of them: I have my mother's sense of high adventure and my father's obsessive work ethic.

As Latter-day Saints, we are enlightened with the glorious knowledge that we are spiritual children of God the Father. We preach it. We sing it. But do we really understand it?

For so long, I didn't.

My life was characterized by chaos. But I never would have fallen so low if I had truly known what it means to be a child of God. I would have reached out for His hand sooner. I would have stood taller and stronger. I never would have believed it was acceptable to allow anyone to abuse me. I would not have neglected or berated myself. I would have found it easier to forgive everyone, especially myself. I would have been more eager to give and more grateful to receive.

Would have. Could have. Should have.

My past cannot be changed, but just because I didn't get a great start does not mean I will be denied a great finish! Life is about change. The greatest change came as I began to understand who I really am and how important the everyday decisions I make are in determining not just who I remain, but who I become.

As I associate with the women of the Church around the world, I'm concerned at how many are discouraged and despondent and how many say they simply "don't care" anymore. They are numb to the pain—which means they are also numb to the joy. I have felt exactly that way, but I promise you that God has a plan and a purpose for your life. His gospel is the only way we can discover who we really are and what our purpose in life is.

"This life is the time for men to prepare to meet God" (Alma 34:32). It won't be easy, and no matter how hard we work we will still fall short. That's why it is paramount to our success and our happiness along the way to realize that Jesus is our Savior and will make up the distance that we cannot go.

WHO VERSUS DO

My question to you, then, is: What is the relationship between our "who" and our "do"? Are we a compilation of what we "do," or are we who we are simply because we are children of the Father?

I have a friend who struggles trying to balance the two. She was born and reared in a Latter-day Saint home. She was loved and nurtured, taught the gospel, and learned right from wrong.

She was baptized and took upon herself promises that she has failed to keep. She's still young, but old enough to know better.

"I'm not blaming anyone but myself," she said, sitting on my sofa one night, drenched in self-loathing. "My sins are mine."

I couldn't help but think how she sounded a bit possessive of "her" sins.

"I've gone too far, done too much. I can never be the person I once was."

"Is that a bad thing?" I asked.

She stopped and stared. "Of course it's a bad thing. I'm supposed to be clean and pure and perfect, like I was when I was a child. Instead I'm filthy and rotten. Even if Jesus did find a way to forgive me, I'd never be the same."

"Exactly. Isn't that all part of the plan?"

"What are you talking about?" she asked.

"Through repentance and the power of the Atonement, what was broken can be mended, but in some very practical ways, I think it can be made stronger than before."

"What do you mean?"

"We came to this earth to learn and grow, to experience things—right?" I asked her.

"Not all things."

"No, not all things, but sin is part of life. Sinning changes us. So does repentance." I thought of King Benjamin's people and their declaration: "The Spirit of the Lord Omnipotent, . . . has wrought a mighty change in us, or in our hearts, that we have no more disposition to do evil, but to do good continually" (Mosiah 5:2).

As we talked into the night, we came to the conclusion that life is all about change. When we had grown and developed and prepared ourselves during our time in our premortal existence we changed by coming to earth, acquiring physical bodies that possessed attributes and appetites. We change as we grow and develop. We are not meant to be sinful creatures, yet sin changes us. But we can repent and be made clean again—stronger, wiser, more empathetic, and better enabled to help.

My friend insisted, "That doesn't mean we should sin just to obtain experience."

"No," I agreed, "just the opposite is true. But I believe that when God helps us past a trial, even when it's through the repentance process, He expects us to use that experience to help strengthen others."

"So you think I can be a child of God again?" she asked.

"I think you've always been a child of God. Nothing changes your spiritual identity."

"But I want to be a better child."

"That is what life is all about, isn't it?"

If we could only see that truth when sin and discouragement and pain and disappointment cloud our vision. President Spencer W. Kimball taught, "All of you need to drink in deeply the gospel truths about the eternal nature of your individual identity and the uniqueness of your personality. You need, more and more, to feel the perfect love which our Father in Heaven has for you and to sense the value he places upon you as an individual. Ponder upon these great truths, especially in those moments when (in the stillness of such anxiety as you may experience as an individual) you might otherwise wonder and be perplexed" ("The Role of Righteous Women," *Ensign,* Nov. 1979, 103).

If our worth should derive not only from our performance, but from our relationship with Christ, how do we get so damned by what we do and do not do? To be damned means to be stopped from progressing. It happens to us when we define ourselves and our worth by our successes and by our failures. When are we going to realize what King Benjamin tried so hard to teach?

> If you should render all the thanks and praise which your whole soul has power to possess, to that God who has created you, and has kept and preserved you, and has caused that ye should rejoice, and has granted that ye should live in peace one with another—
>
> I say unto you that if ye should serve him who has created you from the beginning, and is preserving you from day to day, by lending you breath, that ye may live and move and do according to your own will, and even supporting you from one moment to another—I say, if ye should serve him with all your whole souls yet ye would be unprofitable servants. (Mosiah 2:20–21)

President Joseph Fielding Smith slammed it home when he said: "Do you think it will ever be possible for any one of us, no matter how hard we labor, . . . to pay our Father and Jesus Christ for the blessings we have received from them? The great love, with its accompanying blessings, extended to us through the crucifixion, suffering, and resurrection of Jesus Christ is beyond our mortal comprehension. We never could repay" (*Conference Report,* Apr. 1966, 102).

The Chore Chart

I know a woman who tells a great story that helps me keep this truth in its proper light. She spent weeks crafting a family chore chart, a grid of perfect squares and colors. It occupied a whole wall in her family kitchen so everyone could chart the performance of each member. Do the dishes, get a shiny gold star. Don't do the dishes, get a thick black stripe. Meggy, their youngest daughter, seemed to always acquire more stripes than stars.

Nothing seemed to motivate Meggy to do her assigned chores. She was more interested in following in the footsteps of her hero, the heavyweight boxing gold medalist, Joe Frazier. Unfortunately, Meggy was more of a featherweight, so when she went up against the neighborhood bully, a boy twice her size, Meggy repeatedly came running home with black eyes and bloody noses.

Try as they might, her parents could not seem to focus Meggy away from the neighborhood brawls and onto her chores. There were warnings. There was punishment. But still, there were few stars on that looming chore chart.

One afternoon Meggy's parents were in the kitchen when they heard Meggy scream for help. The bully was after her. "Help, Daddy! I need you!" Meggy's cry was so desperate it rattled the back window.

My friend smiles when she asks, "Did my husband say, 'Let's see how good a girl Meggy has been. Let's count the stars before I go help her'? NO! He did not turn around and even look at the chart. Instead, he tripped over his own legs trying to scramble across the room as fast as he could to reach Meggy. She was his daughter, he was her father, and she was crying for his help!"

I hope the analogy is clear. It's simple. It's natural. It's powerful! God does not withhold His help from us because our performance is imperfect. He runs to help us when we cry out to Him because we are HIS.

IDENTIFYING OUR WORTH

Each of us has a work to accomplish on the earth—chores, if you will. We are here to keep promises we made there. We are here to improve ourselves. As we do our best, in spite of failure and trials, we will begin to grasp our real identity. As we learn about God the Father and Jesus, we will come to better know ourselves. In doing so, we must always keep in mind that we are dual beings, made of both body and spirit.

How do we figure ourselves out? I'm still working hard on that one. It's an ongoing process that requires deep prayer, obedience, and a great sense of adventure to test and try ourselves. President James E. Faust said, "Your strength and identity will come from obeying the commandments, developing your talents, and serving the Lord. Each of you will have to work very hard to qualify for your eternal potential. It will not be easy. Finding your true identity will tax your ability far beyond climbing a dangerous cliff or speeding in a car or on a motorcycle. It will require all of your strength, stamina, intelligence, and courage" ("On the Edge," *New Era*, Feb. 1997, 4).

It's not a game with Heavenly Father. He didn't send us to earth blindfolded with our memories erased, expecting us to grope around in darkness and hopelessness. He sent us with everything we need to find our way back to Him, with everything we need to become like Him. He promises us His help, and He is the only one in this life who will never let us down or disappoint us. He always keeps His promises.

God would not have sacrificed His Son to save us if these two principles were not true: (1) We need saving; and (2) We are *worth* saving.

We all face dark nights when we doubt ourselves. That's when the truths in this book must come to mind: that we are children of the Father, that Jesus is our Savior, that our worth is infinite. If you will take your eyes off yourself and your mind off yourself and put them instead on Christ, I promise you that no matter how dark your nights get, new rays of dawn will find a way to break through the darkness until it dissipates and you can finally and forever see who you really are and what you are worth in the eyes of the Master Creator who created you.

WHO WE CAN BECOME

After life has gone a round or two with you, when you're bloody and beaten and bone weary, it's hard to see clearly or to think like a child of God. It's easy to become disheartened and to feel defeated. President Ezra Taft Benson warned us that the adversary would try to defeat us before we could become the children of God we are capable of becoming: "As the showdown between good and evil approaches with its accompanying trials and tribulations, Satan is increasingly striving to overcome the Saints with despair, discouragement, despondency, and depression" ("Do Not Despair," *Ensign,* Nov. 1974, 2).

The adversary knows that if he can keep us from recognizing our divine potential, he has scored a major victory. Because as long as we fail to recognize that divine potential, we will be held back from achieving all that we can. At my lowest point, all I could think about was what a failure I was. Because I was focused on myself and my pain, I could not see or feel the loving, healing power of Christ.

With Christ, it's not about our past, but our future. He wants us to learn from our mistakes, to live the best we can, and to hope for a bright tomorrow. To be honest, I had no hope for a long time. But as I learned to rely on God's goodness, on Christ's ability to save me, and on my individual worth as a child of God, I have found an inner strength and peace that I did not know existed within me.

Not long after my divorce, I took a hard look around and saw that everything in my world had been neglected. My faith was at an all-time low. Emotionally, I was a wreck. My body was a disaster. My children were more wounded than I was, and they needed all of my help and attention. I had no money. I'd neglected my friends and extended family for years. There wasn't a corner of my outer or inner life that didn't need to be swept out, a single shelf that didn't need repair.

The house we lived in bore the scars of that neglect. I decided it would be good for the children and me to "fix things up." That meant a trip to the hardware store. It took months and many more trips to the store, but eventually we learned to build shelves, to lay tile, to reupholster, to tear down the old in order to build up something new and stronger and better.

A kind neighbor took pity on us and showed up one day with a real tool box. Together, we learned to rewire a broken outlet, to fix a leaky faucet, to plaster over the holes and to make the ugly beautiful. He brushed off our gratitude, saying his effort didn't mean much, but it meant everything to us. For all the while we were painting and sanding and repairing, we were talking and laughing and learning and forging new friendships. Slowly, we were healing.

While we were learning to use drills and saws and caulking guns, God was showing us other tools we had at our disposal— spiritual tools for making spiritual repairs that helped rebuild our broken lives. He showed me that for too long I had simply managed to function, but that we are not here on this earth simply to function; we are here on this earth to LIVE!

I love what Elder Boyd K. Packer said. He reminded us that when we doubt our ability to solve our problems, we haven't yet learned that, as children of an almighty God, we have inherited powerful resources that provide courage and great power (see "Self-Reliance," *Ensign,* Aug. 1975, 88).

Take a minute to assess exactly what you have. For starters, you've got a trio of spiritual tools in your repair kit: faith, hope, and charity. I still promise you the best way to heal your own life is to go out and help to heal someone else's life. As Helen Keller stated, "There is no better way to thank God for your sight than by giving a helping hand to someone in the dark."

When the Spirit whispered over and over to me that I needed to take my focus off myself and put it on my Savior, that meant focusing where His eyes would focus—on someone else in need. Isn't that charity in action? It takes hope that it will all work out, and it takes faith in yourself to step out to represent God.

Dig deep into your spiritual repair kit. I think you'll be surprised at how equipped you really are. Faith gives you focus; hope gives you a reason to keep going. You've got prayer, which is like having a living, breathing instruction guide to every repair you'll ever have to make. You've got the gift of the Holy Ghost for inspiration and coaching. You have the infinite Atonement to rid you of guilt and suffering and sorrow. You've got the power of the priesthood to bless you in every way imaginable. You've got the truth of the scriptures, especially the Book of Mormon, which addresses our lives and our trials today. You've got living prophets and real leaders to correct and encourage you. You've got the temple for refuge.

And you've got laughter. An old Irish proverb says, "A good laugh and a long sleep are the best cures in the doctor's book." We are reminded in the scriptures, "A merry heart maketh a cheerful countenance: but by sorrow of the heart the spirit is broken" (Prov. 15:13).

I love to laugh! I'm not talking about vulgar laughter, but laughter that connects people and elevates everyone's mood. For a long time I couldn't laugh. I couldn't even smile. I'd lost the spiritual tool to enjoy life and to enjoy the people around me.

Make a list of your spiritual tools, and then get down on your knees and plead with heaven to help you master those tools.

No matter how bleak your circumstances, no matter who you were in the past, no matter what you're going through in the present, God can repair your life, He can restore your joy. He can use you to help others. I'm living proof: my circumstances haven't changed, but everything that matters has changed. I know who I am in Christ. No one can ever convince me again that I'm worthless, hopeless, or useless. I'm no longer defined by what others think of me. I have learned to silence that destructive voice that plays in my own head. I now know what Jesus has to say, and it's His voice that I've deemed the definitive voice in my life.

Let Christ Define Your Worth

Consider these facts: Albert Einstein's teacher told his parents that he would never amount to anything of worth. A coaching staff cut Michael Jordan from his high school basketball team. A newspaper editor fired Walt Disney for lacking creativity. Beethoven's piano teacher called him a "hopeless composer." Steven Spielberg was deemed by counselors to be "learning disabled." Winston Churchill failed sixth grade; he was subsequently defeated in every election for public office until he became prime minister at the age of sixty-two. After one of his many defeats, Abraham Lincoln wrote to a friend, "I am now the most miserable man living. If what I feel were equally distributed to the whole human family, there would not be one cheerful face on the earth."

You get the picture. We cannot trust others to determine our worth. We can't even trust ourselves to determine our worth. We have to train ourselves to listen, believe, and act on the only voice that matters—Christ's voice.

He says, "Come follow me." If we do that, we will end up where He is.

Think about that!

I promise you that your worth in God's estimation is infinite. The fact that you are here on this earth at this time is no mistake. You are here now because you were deemed worthy and needed. You have a work to do that no one else on earth can accomplish like you can.

Even when you mess up cataclysmically, there is hope. There is forgiveness. There is a future so bright you'll have to wear megapowered sunglasses just to glimpse it.

Our Father in Heaven and our Savior stand ready to cheer us on, to pick us up when we fall, and to carry us across the finish line if we've worn ourselves out in the cause of the kingdom.

It's time to stop worrying about our worth, to stop measuring ourselves against someone else, to focus instead on the Ultimate Example of both humility and confidence. It's time to stand taller, to smile wider, to live higher, and to follow Christ in doing what He does best: being about His Father's business.

TRUTH #4:
There Is a Plan in Place

Ponder the path of thy feet.
—Proverbs 4:26

I once flew to another city on a last-minute assignment. I was told to hurry and catch the flight and that my itinerary would be emailed to me. I made the flight and arrived at the appointed destination. I checked and rechecked my email. I made phone calls, but couldn't make connections. There I was, ready and willing, but I had no idea what the plan was.

Thankfully, our mortal journey is not without an itinerary. Our Father in Heaven sent us to earth with our itinerary engraved in our hearts. We know why we're here, what our mission is, and how to accomplish that mission. Beyond that, we know most of the details of our return flight home. If we are to stay on course, we cannot allow anyone, especially ourselves, to derail us from the course that was set before we ever left heaven. That doesn't mean there won't be detours and unexpected hazards, because there will be; that doesn't mean there won't be thrilling highs and glorious adventures, because there are supposed to be those things; but as long as we stay tuned in to the Great Navigator—the Holy Spirit—we're guaranteed a safe and successful return.

ACCORDING TO JESUS

Here's the plan laid out in Jesus' own words: "Verily, verily, I say unto you, this is my gospel; and ye know the things that ye must do in my church; for the works which ye have seen me do that shall ye also do; for that which ye have seen me do even that shall ye do" (3 Ne. 27:21).

Wow. All we have to do is live like Jesus, and we'll be just fine.

The sad thing is that none of us—not even those who are truly righteous—can always live to that highest standard. So there is a safety net in place to save us when we fall. It goes by several names. It's called the plan of salvation (see Alma 24:14), because it's there to redeem us when we sell ourselves short. It's called the plan of redemption (see Alma 12:30), because it's there to remind us who we really are and what we're worth in the eyes of the Almighty. It's called the plan of mercy (see Alma 42:15) and the plan of happiness (Alma 42:8), because it's there to wipe away our misery and despair.

The scriptures leave no doubt as to *why* there is a plan in place: to give us our best shot at eternal life, the quality of life that God the Father and Jesus Christ live. They *want* us to have every blessing They have. They want to save us, especially from our own doubts and insecurities and the sins that break our backs and break our hearts.

The very work and glory of God is to "bring to pass the immortality and eternal life of man" (Moses 1:39). Our fundamental work on earth is to gain experience through living—being tested in all things to prove ourselves worthy and obedient.

This is THE PLAN, and it was formulated out of God's love for every single one of His children. How important is it? Elder Neal A. Maxwell answered that question: that of all the errors we could make, the plan of salvation is the one thing we shouldn't be wrong about (see "The Great Plan of the Eternal God," *Ensign,* May 1984, 22).

ALPHA AND OMEGA

In our finite human minds we cannot comprehend the exact beginning of this plan, nor can we understand its eternal endurance. Focus for a moment on the beginning: "Man was also in the beginning with God. Intelligence, or the light of truth, was not created or made, neither indeed can be. . . . For man is spirit. The elements are eternal, and spirit and element, inseparably connected, receive a fullness of joy" (D&C 93:29, 33).

We are not talking about some unknown, indistinguishable matter . . . we are talking about you and me and every other child of God ever created. To focus clearly on our part in the plan, let's go way back. If we don't have an unwavering understanding and conviction of the preexistence, it will be easier for Satan to discourage us about our current existence.

As part of our testing in mortality, we agreed to have a veil drawn over our memories. We're not able to remember what Elder Richard G. Scott calls one of the most exhilarating moments of your life—the moment you learned it was your time to come to earth and experience those things that would prove you victorious (see "First Things First," *Ensign,* May 2001, 6).

Do you *feel* victorious?

I will never forget attending an NBA championship game between the Utah Jazz and the Chicago Bulls. Those of you who recall that game will remember that Michael Jordan had the flu. Reports were that he was so sick he could barely hold his head up. As a Jazz fan, that didn't compel me to compassion. My heart took courage when I actually saw Michael Jordan. He looked sick, pallid, and weak.

I was silently cheering for the flu.

He certainly wasn't on his best game for the first forty minutes. He seemed lethargic—really ill. His forehead beaded with sweat even when he was just sitting on the bench. I saw him glance up at the scoreboard, and for a brief flicker Michael Jordan appeared defeated.

Then something happened. A transformation came over him. His entire body stretched. He tossed a towel to the ball boy and grinned. I saw Michael Jordan make a decision to be victorious.

He looked at the scoreboard again, at the minutes remaining. This time there was fire in Michael's eyes. He did not look to his coach or even to his teammates for approval. The shift of energy came from within him. It was such a powerful transformation that I knew at that moment my basketball team was in dire trouble.

Michael Jordan had a plan. His plan was to win that game no matter the cost.

At some point in our lives we will look up at the scoreboard. We will realize that the shot clock is ticking down, and we will be forced to make a decision—to stay on the bench and give away the game or to get up, get back into the game, and win the whole championship.

Unlike a basketball game, the outcome doesn't depend solely on coaching, refereeing, or even our teammates; the outcome depends on us and how willing we are to follow the game plan that Jesus has laid out for us. He's shown us how to do it. He stands ready to coach and is always cheering and providing everything we need. But it's up to us to get off the bench and get into the game and to play until we win. Remember: our opponent is not another person, but sin. We score against sin every single time we are obedient to the Lord's commands. We score against sin every time we truly repent. We score against evil every time we do good.

Enough of the basketball analogy. This is real life, and there is a plan in place—a perfect plan designed by our Heavenly Father to assure our safe return, but also to ensure that we have the opportunity to a life in mortality that is filled with learning and growth. There is a Cherokee saying that sums this idea up: "When you were born, you cried and the world rejoiced. Live your life so that when you die, the world cries and you rejoice."

It sounds simple, doesn't it? It is simple, but it isn't easy. It wasn't easy for God the Father. It cost Him one-third of his spirit children. It wasn't easy for Jesus Christ. It cost Him suffering beyond what any mortal can fathom. It won't be easy for us . . . but it will be worth it.

Elder John A. Widtsoe wrote, "In our preexistent state, in the day of the great council, we made a[n] . . . agreement with the Almighty. The Lord proposed a plan. . . . We accepted it. Since the plan is intended for all men, we became parties to the salvation of every person under that plan. We agreed, right then and there, to be not only saviors for ourselves but . . . saviors for the whole human family. We went into a partnership with the Lord. The working out of the plan became then not merely the Father's work, and the Savior's work, but also our work. The least of us, the humblest, is in partnership with the Almighty in achieving the purpose of the eternal plan of salvation" ("The Worth of Souls," *The Utah Genealogical and Historical Magazine,* Oct. 1934, 189).

A TWO-PART PLAN

This perfect plan designed for our eternal benefit includes the Creation, the Fall, the Atonement of Christ, and myriad ordinances, commandments, and gospel doctrines. Because I'm a simple girl, I'd like to make this concept simple. I see it as a two-part plan: Christ's part and our part.

Christ did His part by being worthy and humble and willing to become the one and only Savior. When Christ said to our Father, "Here am I. Send me," He volunteered to become the pivotal part in a plan that provides you and me the opportunity to merit eternal life, the very quality life that God Himself lives.

Our part of the plan was to choose between following Christ or Satan. Obviously, we chose to follow Christ. We "shouted for joy" and agreed to fulfill the plan, which required us to leave the presence of our Heavenly Father and to come to earth, without our memories of the premortal existence. We agreed to this physical separation. We agreed to take upon ourselves mortal bodies.

At that point in my existence I must have had a great deal of self-confidence born of my confidence in Christ, because I agreed that I would use my agency to choose to keep God's commandments. I also understood that I would ultimately fail and require a Savior. What became of that confidence? Life has given it a beating, as it does for all of us, but learning and believing what Christ has to say about me is redeeming that confidence. The Apostle Paul encouraged new members of the Church to remember their spiritual experiences and to remain confident in Christ: "Cast not away therefore your confidence, which hath great recompense of reward. For ye have need of patience, that, after ye have done the will of God, ye might receive the promise" (Heb. 10:36).

Our part is to *do* the will of God. Then comes His part: to reward us.

I promise you that when we do our part, God never, ever fails to do His part.

THE LIGHT OF CHRIST

Knowing how much we are loved and valued, it would be ludicrous to think that we would be sent to earth without being properly equipped and prepared to carry out the plan. Every single person born into this world, without exception, has come embedded with a light—the light of Christ. That light helps us make the choices that will lead us home. How we use or abuse that light is part of our testing.

The prophet Mormon teaches, "The Spirit of Christ is given to every man, that he may know good from evil" (Moro. 7:16). The Lord confirmed this truth when he said to the Prophet Joseph Smith that "the Spirit [of Christ] giveth light to every man that cometh into the world; and [that] the Spirit enlighteneth every man through the world, that hearkeneth to the voice of the Spirit" (D&C 84:46).

As baptized and confirmed members of The Church of Jesus Christ of Latter-day Saints, we also have the Holy Ghost to guide us and protect us, to inspire and comfort us.

AGENCY

Inherent in the plan is our ability to choose for ourselves whether or not we will be obedient. President Dieter F. Uchtdorf called the gift of agency one of the greatest gifts from our Father, next to life itself (see "Developing Christlike Attributes," *Ensign,* Oct. 2008, 4).

President Wilford Woodruff said, "God has given unto all of his children . . . individual agency. . . . [We] possessed it in the heaven of heavens before the world was, and the Lord maintained and defended it there against the aggression of Lucifer. . . . By virtue of this agency you and I and all mankind are made responsible beings, responsible for the course we pursue, the lives we live, the deeds we do" (*Millennial Star,* 51:642, in Rulon T. Burton, *We Believe; Doctrines and Principles of the Church of Jesus Christ of Latter-day Saints,* 17).

That means our part is using the light of Christ and the Holy Ghost, using our agency. Our part is to "ponder the path of our feet" and to not wander through life aimlessly, but to move through life with singular purpose: to follow in the footsteps of the Master.

Christ used His agency to offer Himself a sinless sacrifice for sin. There was no other way to cleanse us, because no unclean person can enter into the kingdom of God (see 1 Ne. 15:34). Christ did His part by atoning for more than just our sins. "He hath borne our griefs, and carried our sorrows. . . . He was wounded for our transgressions, he was bruised for our iniquities: the chastisement of our peace was upon him; and with his stripes we are healed" (Isa. 53:4–5).

The Central Part of the Plan

Christ's part was to atone for us, that we might be reconciled to God, be made clean again, and be worthy to enter our Father's presence. Our part is to accept and embrace the saving power of the Atonement.

We accept the terms of the Atonement by exercising faith. To have faith, even extraordinary faith, is not enough. To have faith in someone or something is not enough. We must place our faith in the Only One who will not, who cannot, let us down.

Nothing attests to the love our Heavenly Father has for us more than the Atonement of His Beloved Son Jesus Christ. His part is to invite all to "come unto Christ . . . and partake of his salvation and the power of his redemption" (Omni 1:26).

Our part is to accept that invitation, to believe in that divine love by receiving the saving ordinances that have been restored. We accept Christ's invitation as we remember our promise to be saviors to our brothers and sisters. We do that as we exhibit faith in times of trial. We do that as we endure when it seems impossible to go on—because we do not have to rely on our own goodness, but on Christ's goodness . . . not on our own strength, but on His. What certain others think of us may matter in some ways—but the opinions of others, no matter who they are, should not *define* us. Christ is the audience for whom we perform.

OUR PART

Jesus has done His part. Now we must do ours. President James E. Faust reminds us that we are responsible for our actions, because we have been endowed with the ability to distinguish good from evil—and that the Atonement brings salvation after all we can do (see "The Atonement: Our Greatest Hope," *Ensign,* Nov. 2001, 19–22).

Christ did His part by establishing His gospel while He was in mortality and later restoring it through the Prophet Joseph Smith. We do our part by committing to baptism, accepting the ordinances, learning and studying, belonging and believing, in doing all we can to build up the Church. That includes those who have passed out of this world without having the gospel opportunities we have. The Prophet Joseph said, "The greatest responsibility in this world that God has laid upon us, is to seek after our dead" (*History of the Church,* 6:313).

Christ's part is to provide us with life and the opportunity for an "abundant life." Our part of the plan is to live it to the fullest. Even if you live to be a hundred, life is very short. We can't afford to waste a single day, hour, or minute being negative and ungrateful. The world is intent on flogging us, on stealing our joy. We should never do it to ourselves or to anyone else. We are here to live and to experience all things . . . and to let all experiences tutor us.

What can we do? We can try. We can repent. We can pray. We can endure. We can obey. We can serve. We can testify. We can love. We can teach. We can lift. We can follow a leader who will never lead us astray. But no matter how hard we try, no matter how good we become, we will never be good enough . . . and that's okay. That's been part of the plan from the beginning.

In our Father's plan, there is no place for self-loathing, no room for self-pity. There is no wiggle room for failing to forgive anyone, especially ourselves. There are no corners reserved for hatred or idleness. For the plan to work it must hinge on love and faith and our best works. We must love our God and have faith in Him. We must also love ourselves and have faith in ourselves. When we fail, we must repent sincerely and thoroughly.

Repentance is a vital part of the plan. And for those who suffer because someone else sinned, I beg you to go before the Lord and plead with Him to take away your pain. You'll be amazed at the miracle just waiting for you to receive.

If I've learned anything from being held in the arms of the Savior while I cried, it's that He cries with us. He never stands on the sidelines and scolds. He never belittles or berates us. He heals us. He supports us. He loves us with a love that is so perfect it heals every fracture of our lives.

I don't know exactly where I picked up the wrong thinking that Jesus was disappointed in me. I don't know where I went wrong in believing that God could not love me because I'd messed up. Somehow I thought my pain was due to the fact that I was inadequate and undeserving of joy or security or peace. Oh, the devil had me fooled—every minute that I was wallowing in self-pity and self-loathing, focused on myself, I was not focused on Christ and His power to heal me. Those times were wasted, because those are moments during which I did not progress.

Jesus provided Himself as our Savior. Our part is to allow Him to save us. When we do all we can, He helps carry our burdens—He succors us. He is infinitely able to do that, because He has personally experienced all of it, even our darkest hours.

Our part is to not forget or neglect ourselves or anyone else. Christ did His part by setting a perfect example of how we should live, to love the Lord with all our heart, might, mind, and soul, and to love our neighbors as we love ourselves (see Matt. 22:37–39).

God's love is not something we can earn, no matter how hard we try or how high we run up the scoreboard. God's love is "freely given" to all who will believe, come unto Christ, and endure.

Christ never fails us, but because we are mortal, we are going to fail Him from time to time. When we do, we have to believe— not in our own failing, but in His goodness, His compassion, and His mercy. I promise you that this great plan in which we are taking part is a plan of hope.

When I found myself in great difficulty in my life, I had no ability to stop the difficulties. But when I called out for help, the strong arm of my Savior was fast and ready to catch me and protect me. It's what Jesus does best.

The Atonement seems like it happened so long ago—more than two thousand years ago—but in a very real sense our part of that great plan happens every time we call out for Jesus to save us, every time we "come unto Christ," whenever we renew our covenants, whenever we truly repent and offer as our part a broken heart and a contrite spirit.

It's hard to feel worthy to "come unto Christ" when we've been soiled by sin or torn to shreds by the blades of adversity, but the truth is this: in the final analysis, we are all unworthy. But God is not eager to punish and cause pain. Just the opposite is true.

I will never forget walking through the Church of the Holy Sepulchre in Jerusalem. For those around me the experience seemed to be one of passion and intense spirituality. For me it was torture. The building loomed dark and confusing. People were weeping and wailing, some even flailing themselves onto the floor. Candles were burning, and the air was thick with smoke and soot. There were sections of the walls that were covered in vile graffiti. I found it hard to breathe and wandered away from the crowds, down a corridor all by myself. I struggled to feel what I was supposed to feel and berated myself for not "getting" what seemed so obvious to everyone else. Then I looked up and saw a huge portrait of Jesus Christ. It was dark and old and peeling in places. A scowling Savior was depicted sitting on a high-backed throne, a haloed crown on his head, a velvet robe around his shoulders, a globe of the world in one hand and a whip in the other.

My heart broke wide open.

This—a god of fierce judgment and eager punishment—was not the Jesus I had come to know. This was not the Lord who loved us so much that He freely gave His life, bleeding from every pore to atone for our sins and our sufferings. This was not the Savior who had come to me, who had held me in His arms and wept with me. This was not the Jesus Christ who begs us all, "Come unto me."

I don't think I've ever felt such sorrow or borne a heavier heart than I did while standing there beneath that unfamiliar Christ— not because I felt bad for me, but because I felt bad for Jesus. Jesus, the God of light and life and love, is perceived by so many of us not as *He* is, but as *we* are: dark, despairing, vengeful, hard, and even brutal. In the very presence of the portrait I felt sadder than I'd ever felt.

This was not the Christ that Isaiah prophesied "will abundantly pardon" (Isa. 55:7). This was not the Jesus who promised, "In the world ye shall have tribulation: but be of good cheer; I have overcome the world" (John 16:33). This dark, distorted Messiah certainly wasn't the "light that is endless, that can never be darkened" (Mosiah 16:9).

Adversity Is Not Punishment

Among the lessons I learned from that soul-ripping experience is this: our trials in life are not meant to harm us, but to help raise us up. We knew before agreeing to come to earth that we would face adversity here but that we would *not* be left alone. Christ has agreed to be with us "always."

Christ did His part by finishing the work He'd been given to do by His Father. "Though he were a Son, yet learned he obedience by the things which he suffered. And being made perfect, he became the author of eternal salvation unto all them that obey him" (Heb. 5:8–9).

If we are to do our part, we cannot give up when trials are toughest. Compared to Christ's sufferings, we have suffered nothing.

Maybe, just maybe, all my pain and suffering wasn't because I was worthless or because I was "in trouble" with God. Maybe my trials were something more and something very different than I'd supposed. Maybe they were a way to bring me closer to my Lord and Savior.

Don't misunderstand. I do not believe for one minute that God wanted our little family to suffer the abuse that we did, but I do believe that what Satan meant to harm us, God can turn to good. Maybe, just maybe, all our pain can be transformed into a testimony that we can share with others who are also suffering.

I think of one of my friends. I stood beside her in the temple when she was married. I held her hand as she gave birth to her daughters. I offered a shoulder when her husband left her and their daughters to live with another man. I wiped tears from her cheeks when her oldest daughter committed suicide, when her middle daughter nearly died from a drug overdose, and when her youngest daughter abandoned her faith. Three nights ago I listened as my friend bore witness to me in words that lifted my spirit. "Everything—and I mean *everything*—I've gone through has brought me closer to my Savior. Would I ask for such suffering? Never. But would I trade it for the relationship I've built with Jesus? Never. He knows my name and my pain and He has shown up whenever I have needed Him the most."

That's how I feel. I would not trade anything for the absolute testimony that I have now. I know Jesus is our Savior. I know that He wants to save us. I know that He can save us if we will allow Him to. Suffering is not punishment, but a means to spiritual progress.

Orson F. Whitney made sense of suffering: "No pain that we suffer, no trial that we experience is wasted. It ministers to our education, to the development of such qualities as patience, faith, fortitude and humility. All that we suffer and all that we endure, especially when we endure it patiently, builds up our characters, purifies our hearts, expands our souls, and makes us more tender and charitable, more worthy to be called the children of God . . . and it is through sorrow and suffering, toil and tribulation, that we gain the education that we come here to acquire and which will make us more like our Father and Mother in heaven" (in Spencer W. Kimball, *Faith Precedes the Miracle* [Salt Lake City: Deseret Book Co., 1972], 98).

Our eyes cannot see what God can see. "Ye cannot behold with your natural eyes, for the present time, the design of your God concerning those things which shall come hereafter, and the glory which shall follow after much tribulation. For after much tribulation come the blessings" (D&C 58:3–4).

If the Savior could save me, then no matter who you are or where you are, no matter what you've done or what's been done to you, Jesus knows and is ready and anxious to love you and to redeem you.

It's all part of a plan that we agreed to, a glorious but simple two-part plan that cannot fail if we do our part—because Jesus Christ will never fail to do His.

TRUTH #5:

Satan Is Out to Destroy Us

Be sober, be vigilant; because your adversary the devil,
as a roaring lion, walketh about, seeking whom he may devour.
—1 Peter 5:8

When I was young and first heard about the war in heaven, I felt pity for Satan. After all, he made a bad mistake and the gospel is all about giving people second chances. Couldn't he just repent and be set right with God again?

I used to feel sorry until I got to know Satan, and I realized that he did not make a mistake. He made a choice: a choice to rebel against our Father in Heaven, a choice to try to destroy God's kingdom.

He is still not sorry and never will be. He is a son of destruction, and his cunning and selfishness cost our Father one-third of all His spirit children—our spirit brothers and sisters. I'm the mother of six children. The thought of losing two of them to the dark side is beyond my comprehension.

I no longer feel sorry for Satan because I know now that Satan doesn't feel sorry for me. His goal in the beginning was to destroy our happiness and our chance for eternal life with our families. That goal has not changed one bit. He's just had a lot more practice at being destructive—and, frankly, he's also had a lot more success at it.

We need to completely understand a very hard truth: Satan wants to destroy us, to destroy our children, to destroy everything that is good in this life. He will use any person or any tactic to harm us. He is evil to the very core. The battle he began in heaven rages here on earth: "Satan stirreth them up, that he may lead their souls to destruction. And thus he has laid a cunning plan, thinking to destroy the work of God; . . . And . . . he . . . leadeth them along until he draggeth their souls down to hell; . . . And thus he goeth up and down, to and fro in the earth, seeking to destroy the souls of men" (D&C 10:22–23, 26–27).

Don't say you haven't been warned!

Whenever my teenage boys head out the front door, I tell them, "Remember who you are." They laugh and roll their eyes, replying, "It's you, Mom, who forgets stuff."

Oh, how Satan wants us to forget stuff. The important stuff. Like who God is, who Jesus Christ is, and who we are in the great plan of happiness.

He wants us to think that we are insignificant, inadequate, that we just don't matter. He wants to convince us that we have messed our lives up so appallingly that there is no hope for redemption. He wants us to believe that bad things happen to us because we deserve them, because God doesn't love us.

Elder Richard G. Scott made it clear when he taught that Satan will strive to alienate us from our Heavenly Father by convincing us that our Father can't love us—or He wouldn't allow tragic things to happen to us. Such a line of thinking, Elder Scott reminds us, is a lie, and if we fall victim to it, we have allowed ourselves to be "manipulated by Satan" (see "To Heal the Shattering Consequences of Abuse," *Ensign*, May 2008, 40–43).

What did Elder Scott say? He told us that if we believe Heavenly Father doesn't love us, we are being manipulated by Satan. Write that advice on a card; write it on a dozen cards if you must, and put them around so you can be reminded by whose definition your identity and worth are determined!

God has a plan, and you are part of that plan. So is Satan. Did you know that *Satan* is the Hebrew name for "devil"? He is also called "Lucifer" and "the father of all lies." He's smart. Gordon B. Hinckley called him "clever and subtle" ("Don't Drop the Ball," *Ensign,* Nov. 1994, 46). I've come to realize that if I am not spiritually educated, aware, and in tune with the Holy Ghost, it's a piece of cake for Satan to lie to me, confuse me, discourage me, and even destroy me.

Just as we have to know God the Father and Jesus Christ in order to navigate successfully through life, we have to know that Satan is our eternal enemy if we are to avoid the deadly traps that he sets for us. We have to know who Satan is, what he wants, and how he works. This knowledge is monumental is helping us protect our sense of self. Satan revels in playing head games. He twists and taints our thoughts. It always begins with a thought.

This book is all about changing our thoughts from destructive deceits to constructive truths. It's about silencing Satan and listening to Jesus. We do that by replacing wrong thoughts with right thoughts. Right thinking leads to right acting. We change our thoughts and we change our actions, and that's when we change our lives.

Satan knows that. He wants to control our thoughts because then he can control us. Along with our agency, we have been warned that our thoughts make us what we are—so if we want to become like Christ, we must think Christlike thoughts (see Ezra Taft Benson, "Think on Christ," *Ensign,* Mar. 1989, 2).

Now that you know that Satan wants inside your mind, you're the only one with agency to kick him out of that "head game."

KNOW WHO SATAN IS

All of us, including Satan, are spirit sons and daughters of God. Those of us who live in mortality "shouted for joy" when our Father's plan was presented. There were others, led by Satan, who did not. Perhaps they lacked faith in Father, in His plan, or in themselves. No matter; they actively opposed the plan and worked relentlessly to destroy the agency we possessed then and possess now. In Satan's own words, "I will redeem all mankind, that one soul shall not be lost, and surely I will do it; wherefore give me thine honor" (Moses 4:1).

The details of our premortal memories are temporarily veiled. But we know from scripture that Satan "sought to destroy the agency of man" (Moses 4:3). Satan's plan would damn us from the beginning—stop us from progressing, confine us to the same plane eternally. Under Satan's plan we would remain stagnant; there would be no learning, no growth, no development. Where is the challenge in that?

Take heart! Obviously, we had faith in ourselves and in our Father, who wants to challenge us, so we could grow and progress and become like Him. We were taught the plan of salvation and allowed to decide for ourselves. It wasn't an easy decision. But we made that decision when we used our agency to vote in favor of Father's plan.

The scriptures teach us that Satan had brilliance and influence. He was loved by Father. He held a position of authority.

But he rebelled when his plan of control and selfishness was rejected. One-third of our spirit brothers and sisters vowed their allegiance to him. Under Father's order they were cast out, denied mortal bodies, and damned by their own decision. "And he became Satan, yea, even the devil, the father of all lies, to deceive and to blind men, and to lead them captive at his will, even as many as would not hearken unto my voice" (Moses 4:4).

Satan lives just as surely as we do. The world likes to teach that there really isn't a devil—that evil is just an idea created to manipulate us. Go read the most popular self-help books, ones that sell millions of copies; they profess that "there is no devil."

Wrong!

There *is* a devil. It is no coincidence that the devil has the world shouting that he is not real while he tells the same lie about God. Remember Korihor from the Book of Mormon? Alma records Korihor's confession after Satan brought him to the point of utter destruction: "Behold, the devil hath deceived me; for he appeared unto me in the form of an angel, and said unto me: . . . There is no God; yea, and he taught me that which I should say. And I have taught his words; . . . and I taught them, even until I had much success, . . . that I verily believed that they were true; and for this cause I withstood the truth even until I have brought this great curse upon me" (Alma 30:53).

Do not be deceived. Satan and his followers are real. Their power is real. We have to educate ourselves and teach our loved ones the monumental difference between Satan and our Savior— that "all things which are good cometh of God; and that which is evil cometh of the devil; for the devil is an enemy unto God, . . . and inviteth and enticeth to sin" (Moro. 7:12).

President Spencer W. Kimball gave the following description of Satan: "Satan is very much a personal, individual spirit being, but without a mortal body. His desires to seal each of us his are no less ardent in wickedness than our Father's are in righteousness to attract us to his own eternal kingdom. . . . He is also clever and trained. With thousands of years of experience behind him he has become superbly efficient and increasingly determined" (*The Miracle of Forgiveness* [Salt Lake City: Bookcraft, 1969], 21).

If you're thinking that you are inferior, that your best will never be good enough, that your life is ruined beyond repair, please know that any thought to diminish your worth—whether it comes from your own mind or the mouth of someone else—is not of God.

It's important to know that out of His love for us and His trust in us, Heavenly Father allows Satan and his followers to tempt us, to try us. It is part of our mortal experience (see 2 Ne. 2:11–14; D&C 29:39). God wants us to know the truth of all things; that's why He has given us the Holy Ghost, a spirit of truth to guide and protect us. Use the Holy Ghost's power to discern light from lies. Use the power of the Holy Ghost to help you recognize Satan and avoid his deadly traps.

WHAT SATAN WANTS

Satan wants us to be as miserable as he is. It's that simple. It's that sick. "He seeketh that all men might be miserable like unto himself" (2 Ne. 2:27). Satan wants to deceive us. After Adam had taught his posterity the gospel, Satan told them, "Believe it not; and [for the most part] they believed it not" (Moses 5:13).

He wants to have what you have: a mortal body and the chance at eternal life. Since he knows that is impossible, he wants you. He "desireth to have you" (3 Ne. 18:18). He gets his evil wish as he gets you to break the law of chastity, lie, steal, destroy others, or destroy yourself.

Satan wants to stop you from praying (see 2 Ne. 32:8). He knows there is tremendous power available through prayer, so he will tell any lie he has to in order to keep you from calling on your Father in Heaven for help.

I met a beautiful young woman at BYU. Her future was blindingly bright. She graduated with a nursing degree and had her mission papers turned in. One night while she was locking the office where she worked a man came up behind her, wrestled her to the ground, and assaulted her. During the struggle the knife used to terrify her sliced deeply beneath her chin. The man fled, thinking he'd cut her throat.

Those of us close to her were shocked and devastated. The physical wounds healed, but the inner scars remained sore and infected. She became bitter toward God. Why hadn't He protected her when all of her life she had honored Him? None of us had a satisfactory answer. Even her parents seemed to lose faith.

Her mission was delayed and finally abandoned. The young men who invited her to date were turned down. Even with professional counseling, she pulled away into a world of her own until one day she announced that she was moving across the country where no one knew her story.

For a long time we remained in contact until her letters and phone calls finally quit coming. I thought of her, just found her this last year. I haven't aged that gracefully either, but this woman looked old and beaten. She laughed bitterly when I told her that yes, I was still a member of the Church and still convinced of the truth of the gospel.

She called me a fool. She said I had been brainwashed, bludgeoned into thinking that God cared when she knew for a fact that He doesn't. She did her best to try to convince me that our Heavenly Father is not involved in our lives. She claimed that He couldn't care less. She was eloquent and practiced in her delivery. But when she could see that it wasn't going to work on me, she turned away, concluding, "God might exist, but He doesn't care what happens to His children."

As she turned away, the side of her thumb brushed beneath her chin, caressing a scar that reminded her of a lifetime of pain and suffering. I couldn't help thinking how Jesus aches to heal her wounds, to hold her in His arms and bring light into the dark world she inhabits.

I couldn't help thinking how Satan wants to alienate us from our Father in Heaven and His Son's saving grace and healing power. He wants us to think that we are alone in our struggles.

Satan wants us to lose the companionship of the Holy Ghost—our guide, our comfort, and our protector. Pray for the companionship of the Holy Ghost. "Pray always that you may come off conqueror" (D&C 10:5).

How Satan Works

How does Satan do it? He is quite straightforward and predictable. First, he attempts to prompt doubts in our minds about our divine potential. He even cultivates doctrine in the world implying we are much less than we really are. He undermines our faith—and thus our confidence—in our ability to achieve our potential. He strives to bring us to a mindset in which we believe that we, individually, are not good enough to ever achieve our celestial goals.

Elder Jeffrey R. Holland asked who it is that whispers to us that the gifts given to others and the achievements others make somehow diminish us—somehow take away from the blessings we have received. He reminds us that it is none other than Satan, the father of all lies, the one who asked that the glory be given him (see "The Other Prodigal," *Ensign,* May 2002, 62).

There are people in my life who edify me with their presence. They make me want to be a better person. They bring me closer to Christ. These are instruments in the hands of God. There are also people—people I love—who find subtle ways to wear me down and tear me down. They make me doubt myself and draw away from Christ. These are instruments in the hands of Satan. President Joseph Fielding Smith warned us that Satan may influence us through friends, relatives, or other people in whom we have confidence (see *Melchizedek Priesthood Course of Study,* 1972–73, 298).

Satan has an endless bag of tricks, so many I can't tell you what they are, but I can address the tactics he uses. He uses fear. As a little girl I remember lying awake at night, fearing that my mother might die and leave me.

Guess what?

She died and left me.

Eleanor Roosevelt wrote, "You gain strength, courage and confidence by every experience in which you really stop to look fear in the face. You are able to say to yourself, 'I have lived through this horror. I can take the next thing that comes along.'"

I can testify to the truth in that statement.

The Lord Himself has said, "If ye are prepared ye shall not fear" (D&C 38:30).

I wasn't prepared. I wasn't prepared to lose a parent or my marriage. I wasn't prepared to discover that my children had been injured and that the depth of their wounds could not be measured. I wasn't prepared to realize that so much of the future I'd saved and worked and invested in was gone and was never coming back.

The devil laughed. He lied when he told me that there was no hope left—that I had no future, that my children had no future. He convinced me that if I wasn't such an idiot I would have seen this all coming. And while I was believing his lies, he came against me with fear. He wanted me to fall apart, to fall down and never get back up.

He had me right where he wanted me—for a time. But slowly, the Lord's light cast out the darkness. Truth overcame lies. Faith overcame fear.

My fears did not leave. I had to move forward, trying, even though I was afraid. I had to move through it. Winston Churchill wisely said, "If you are going through hell, keep going."

What kept me going was constant prayer and trying to follow any hint of inspiration I felt. I made it a point to study the scriptures and everything the Lord said about fear. I read every conference talk on fear and how to conquer it—every single talk. In my prayers I begged for freedom from fear. When I discovered that fear is the opposite of faith and that they cannot coexist, Satan made me feel guilty, telling me that I had no faith. But the Lord gently taught me, "There is no fear in love; but perfect love casteth out fear; because fear hath torment" (1 Jn. 4:18–19).

I was worried by so many questions. Then, like He always does, the Lord added a higher level to my learning. *Keep reading,* the Spirit whispered. I went back to the fourth chapter of 1 John: "If a man say, I love God, and hateth his brother, he is a liar . . . for he who loveth God love his brother also" (vv. 20–21).

If I wanted to get rid of the fear, I had to replace it with love. "Perfect love" the scripture says, "casteth out fear."

My ability to love was far from perfect.

This is where the story gets really exciting, because this is where the power of the Atonement of Christ comes in. I was too human to love with any degree of perfection, but I could receive perfect love by the One who loves without error.

It was Halloween time, and the Lord had a lesson to teach me about receiving love. The doorbell rang and I greeted a porch crammed with children, dressed in costumes, shouting at once, "Trick or treat!"

I held out my cauldron of goodies and eager little hands went in one after another, dipping to grab their favorite candy bar. When they were satisfied I looked up to see two parents standing toward the back. I held that same cauldron out to them.

They both backed up, held up straight hands, and said, "Oh, no. We can't."

"Why not?" I asked. "We've got Snickers, Milky Way bars, and Almond Joys. There are even some Hershey chocolate bars."

"Oh," said one woman, "Almond Joys are my favorite."

"Good. Take two," I urged.

She stepped forward, her hand went out, but then she recoiled.

"I can't. Thanks, but I just can't take a candy bar. I don't deserve one."

Deserve one? I was baffled. It was an offering . . . a gift. There was no *deserving* required.

But the adults backed off the porch and followed the happy children into the darkness. As I closed the door I realized that's how we often are. The Lord is holding out His love, anxious for us to receive it, but we're stepping away, saying we don't deserve it. We refuse to accept it.

Please don't think that I have spiritual promptings every Halloween! On that occasion, though, I did. It was only when I learned to *receive* God's love that I began to get rid of the fear. I again changed the way I prayed. I started to thank God for His love, love He had demonstrated for me and for my children all along. When I stepped out into the warm rays of the sunshine or the hard rain of a storm or even the soft snow, I looked up and thanked God for His love.

It wasn't easy. I was used to apologizing, making promises to be better. It did not feel natural, but I've lived long enough to know that we cannot proceed through life based on feelings. We have to do what is right no matter how we feel. At first I felt like an idiot. But eventually it began to feel right. I began to recognize God's perfect love, and I received it even though I was, and am, far from perfect.

That is when abiding faith in Jesus Christ began to replace the fears that had wrecked havoc in my life. And only then—only when I had received love—could I give love away, because you can't give away something you don't have.

How to Silence Satan

Facing down evil is not easy, but we have more power than we think. We don't need to run away when we feel fear; we need to stand firm, strong, and tall.

That power means power to face the real truth: that everything amiss in our lives is not the devil's doing. I had responsibility for my own choices; we all do. We need to take on responsibility, strengthen the good within us, and overcome the temptations of

Satan. The direction-finder is sure. Alma tells us, "Whatsoever is good cometh from God, and whatsoever is evil cometh from the devil" (Alma 5:40).

I began to replace the devil's lies with the Lord's truths. Now I have no doubt about what my Father in Heaven and Christ think of me, because they've told me through the scriptures and through the Spirit. I know that they don't lie. They know my heart. They know my sins and my sufferings. And I'm beginning to know them through the power of prayer, through the whisperings of the Holy Ghost, and through the literal power of the Word of God. It wasn't until I did battle with Satan after the manner that Jesus battled Satan that I began to claim victory.

Oh, that devil is a low life. There are two times he attacks us: when we are doing what's wrong and when we're doing what's right. When we are doing what's wrong, being disobedient, offending the Spirit, we invite the destroyer into our lives. But what about the times we're doing our best to keep the commandments? You might think Satan would leave us alone.

Nope. That's not going to happen.

One morning I went to an early session at the temple. I felt a strong presence of the Spirit and came out feeling fortified and edified, but as I crossed the street to attend a meeting at the Missionary Training Center, I felt an opposite spirit attack me. It seemed to come out of nowhere, and before I was able to arrive at my destination, any strength or happiness I'd experienced was gone. I didn't understand. I'd been doing what was right, yet still this attack came against me.

There is no better example of this point than the one provided by the Savior. In the fourth chapter of Matthew we picture a Christ who has separated Himself from the world to better commune with His Father. Satan waits patiently as forty days and forty nights tick by. He waits with eager anticipation, because Satan's strategy is to come against us when we are at our most vulnerable. Hungry and tired. Discouraged and doubtful. I do not know the state of Christ's mind at that time, but I know that physically He was famished, His body was weak, and He was in dire need of physical nourishment.

Pay close attention to the first thing the devil did. He tried to make Jesus doubt His own identity, His infinite worth. "*If* thou be the Son of God . . . command that these stones be made bread" (Matt. 4:3; emphasis added).

Notice that he tried to get Christ to doubt Himself, and in the same sentence, Satan appealed to the human appetite: "You're hungry, let's get you some bread." He also tempted Jesus to use His godly powers for earthly gain: "*If* you're the Son of God, use your power to feed your appetite."

What did Jesus do? He quoted scripture! "It is written, Man shall not live by bread alone but by every word that proceedeth out of the mouth of God" (Matt. 4:4).

Don't you just love that? Jesus quoted scripture to the devil. What a lesson for us!

Again, when they were on a pinnacle, Satan tried his strategy again: "*If* thou be the Son of God . . ." (Matt. 4:6; emphasis added).

What did Jesus do? Again, He quoted scripture: "It is written again, Thou shalt not tempt the Lord thy God" (Matt. 4:7).

Hold the bus! Back up and read that again. I don't want you to miss the point. Jesus did something more in this confrontation on which we usually fail to focus. Jesus not only spoke back to the devil by quoting scripture, He also bore witness to Satan of His own identity. Jesus *knew* He was the Son of God, and He knew Satan knew it.

I'm not suggesting in any way or form that we invite a conversation with Satan. Never. But what would happen in our lives if, when the devil comes against us, trying to make us doubt our identity and value, that we talk back to him—if we shut him up the same way Jesus did? Our weapon is the word of God. We have to know it so that we can use it to bear witness to ourselves and to our enemy that we are children of God with power and purpose and unbounded value.

In the end, Satan offered Jesus all that he has to offer—the riches and power of one planet. In comparison to what God offers, it was pitiful and meaningless.

"Then saith Jesus unto him, Get thee hence, Satan: *for it is written,* Thou shalt worship the Lord thy God, and him only shalt thou serve" (Matt. 4:10; emphasis added).

Jesus bore testimony of the Father and testified to the force of His love.

It worked for Jesus and it worked for me. It will work for you too, as you replace Satan's lies with God's truths.

Again, I am *not* suggesting that we negotiate with Satan. There is no room for negotiation at the altar of the adversary. We should *never* do anything to invite the devil or entice him, but when he makes the first move, we have the power to counter him. It is paramount that we do not believe the lies he tells; when self-destructive thoughts come, they can be combated with the power of God's word.

It's not easy, and it takes a great deal of time, effort, and dedication, but the rewards are without measure.

The Power to Overcome Is Ours

Isn't it wonderful to know that we can silence Satan with the word of God? That God is always on our side? President Hinckley promised, "You have His power within you to sustain you. You have the right to call upon God to protect you. . . . Stand your ground and hold your place, and you will be triumphant. As the years pass, you will look back with satisfaction upon the battles you have won in your individual lives" ("Overpowering the Goliaths in Our Lives," *Ensign,* Jan. 2002, 2).

My young son likes to run. He runs fast and forward. I worry that one day he will run into danger, so I have taken him out to the road again and again and taught him to look both ways before he crosses the street. I've probably done this a hundred times.

The other day we were by his school, on a busy street near a busy parking lot, and I called out to him, "Look before you cross the street, son."

He stopped and cranked his head to the left and then to the right. Then to the left and back to the right. He looked back at me. He then turned all the way around. I saw his dark eyes go big.

"What's wrong?" I called.

"Which way do I look first? Danger is coming from all directions!"

He is right on. Danger is coming at us from all directions. We live in a world and at a time when Satan and his demons are unleashed and relentless. They'll stop at nothing to destroy us. The good news is that we have a promise from the One who never breaks His promises that we will never be tempted beyond our ability to resist.

We know that God "will never allow Satan to go too far. Satan and his aides no doubt may know our inclinations, our carnal tastes and desires, but they cannot compel a righteous person to do evil if he seeks help from the Lord" (Marilyn Arnold, "Questions and Answers," *New Era,* Jul. 1975, 46–47).

But Satan will lead us to the very edge and then push us over when our guard is down. I hope to be extraordinarily sensitive to this issue, but I have to testify to you that there is no such thing as a "little sin." Sin is sin, no matter how small or pretty the package. Satan will lie and tell us, "One time is just one time." But one time leaves the gate wide open for the next time.

I know without doubt that the power and love of the Atonement can heal you of sin. There is light after the dark. I promise you that if you will search, ponder, and pray about the truths that come from Christ, if you will let Him define your worth and your future, everything—and I mean everything—will get better and brighter.

Do not lose faith in your Father in Heaven or in yourself. You are not alone. You are not the problem. Satan is. You have access to the greatest power there is—God's healing power through the Atonement of Jesus Christ. Take advantage of that power.

The Prophet Joseph Smith understood how we blame and punish ourselves and how that can lead to a living hell: "A man is his own tormentor and his own condemner. . . . The torment of disappointment in the mind of man [or woman] is as exquisite as a lake burning with fire and brimstone" (*Deseret News,* 8 July 1857, 138).

Remember what Alma experienced when he made it "through" that hell: "My soul hath been redeemed from the gall of bitterness and bonds of iniquity. I was in the darkest abyss; but now I behold the marvelous light of God. My soul was racked with eternal torment; but . . . my soul is pained no more" (Mosiah 27:29).

If you need to repent, and we all do, then repent. Do it without delay and do it completely. When you are clean, I beg you to stay pure and clean . . . do not listen when Satan invites you to inch toward the edge just to look over and see what sin looks like. Stay as far away from the edge as you can get!

The power of the Atonement is not just for sinners. It's equally meant to ease the burdens of those who suffer. Lay your burden at the altar of Christ's feet. He will pick it up and carry it for you. He will pick you up and carry you if that's needed, too. It's what He does. It's what He wants to do. He loves you with a love that transcends any kind of emotion we can fathom.

I testify to you from the depths of my soul that you are loved. You have power to resist Satan and to heal from the wounds that he inflicts. When Joseph Smith, at the age of fourteen, went into the grove to pray, the first thing that happened when he opened his mouth was that the power of the adversary tried to terrify him and crush him, tried to silence him. But what did Joseph do? He prayed through it! We can do that, too.

REMEMBER

We can keep a record of all the good things that God does for us so that we can be reminded that God's power is greater than Satan's. It really aggravates and hinders Satan when we keep records of God's good deeds to prove that we are loved, blessed, and remembered by the Lord.

We can learn the word of God and use it as a weapon to defeat the devil. "Thy Word have I hidden in my heart, that I might not sin against thee" (Ps. 119:11). This means we are called to really get up and be about our Father's business, not to sit idle and allow Satan to put thoughts into our heads. Remember what

Moroni wrote to Pahoran: "Do ye suppose that the Lord will still deliver us, while we sit upon our thrones and do not make use of the means which the Lord has provided for us?" (Alma 60:21).

We can silence Satan. We are children of the Great Parent of the Universe. We belong to Him. His Son has atoned for our sins and our sorrows. The key is to believe in God's goodness and not in our own failures. As we repent and do our best to keep the commandments, His power will become our power. No matter what fiery darts the devil shoots our way, no matter where they hit, or how deep they sink, we can be healed. *We can be made whole again.*

If we do our part, God will never fail to do His. In the end our promise is sure: "He that overcometh shall inherit all things; and I will be his God, and he shall be my son" (Rev. 21:7).

TRUTH #6:

There Is Power within Us

My peace I give unto you: not as the world giveth, give I unto you.
Let not your heart be troubled, neither let it be afraid.
—John 14:27

As I travel and have opportunities to speak to women both in and out of the Church, I ask what they want most in life. No matter their home or their language, I continually hear the same two answers: "I want to feel happy. I want to live in peace."

Isn't that the universal quest?

Peace and happiness.

There are certain things that just go together, and one would not be complete without the other.

Salt and pepper.

Joseph and Mary.

Sand and sea.

Peace and happiness are two of those things. And even though we might glimpse our true selves from time to time, there is no way we can maintain a consistent realm of wholeness unless there is peace and happiness in our lives. Peace gives us a sense of security in times of trial, and happiness is found in investing ourselves in the truths that last.

Unless we know what Jesus says about peace and happiness, it's a sure bet we'll get caught up in the lies of the world.

Self-gratification, glitter, gold, and gluttony all promise us peace and happiness, but only Christ can deliver the real deal.

There was a time in my life when peace was a foreign concept to me. I barely smiled. It was difficult for me to look people in the eye. There was a heaviness in my heart that dragged me through life with no passion, no color, no hope.

I felt absolutely alone.

I wanted to redefine my life. I wanted faith. I wanted peace. I ached to feel happy.

I remember getting up one fall morning determined that I would do what Moses did—I'd go to the mountain to pray! There I would find God, and He would lift from my bended shoulders the weight that threatened to break me. At the top of the mountain was where I would find peace and happiness. Did I ever have a plan! Because it was fall, I thought I'd enjoy the palette the Lord uses to paint the changing of the seasons. There amidst the golds, reds, and oranges of autumn I'd beg God for peace and happiness. I'd stay up there until I received the help that I sought.

My plan would have worked, if only I'd planned a little better.

I simply announced to my family, "Mom needs a little alone time. I'm going on a solo drive, and I'll be back when I get back."

I was such a jumbled case of emotions, I drove without direction. I live in a land of mountains, so I didn't much care which one I chose. My mind reeled with doubts and fears. I cried until my eyes were nearly swollen shut—not a good condition when you're navigating the freeway. When I realized how far south I had gone, I pulled off the exit by Payson, Utah. Then I remembered—Payson has a spectacular canyon. In my oblivious brilliance, I started toward the entrance but found myself lodged in a long line of traffic. The congestion frustrated me.

I thought there might be an accident ahead or a construction project. Why else would the streets be so crowded on an autumn Saturday in Payson, Utah?

If I'd only taken the focus off my own worries and looked up, I would have seen the GIANT billboard announcing that this particular Saturday was set aside to celebrate PAYSON'S ONION DAYS GRAND PARADE!

That's right. The whole town was assembled to celebrate onions, and there I was, pulling my car into a winding line of traffic that I thought would lead me back out of the city. Silly me. What I'd really done was pull my car into the line of floats and automobiles, horses and juggling clowns, all poised and ready to *enter* the parade!

A shimmering float with the local dairy princesses was right in front of my car, and the local marching band was lining up behind me, tubas blaring. You can imagine my panic. My horror. I had to get out of there, but there was no wiggle room. I'd joined the line, and a waving man was ordering me to keep it going and to not slow down the festivities.

I rolled down my window and shouted a frantic explanation at him, but he just waved his wand to keep the parade entrants moving. You can imagine the amount of peace I felt at that moment.

There had to be some way for me to weasel out. What could I do? I inched my car into place, amid the music and the cheers, sliding so far down into the seat that I could barely see through the windshield, but I could see both sides of Main Street lined with people cocking their heads and squinting. Little children were elbowing their parents, no doubt asking, "How come she's in the parade?"

Parents shrugged, baffled. My car was white—no decorations, no business logo. I was just a crazy woman driving a big old plain white car. I drove three entire blocks like that. It seemed like three years before I found a packed side street and veered off, making people scatter out of my way.

I will never forget driving home. At first I beat myself up for being such a blind idiot. I looked over at the mountain I'd missed. The whole span was awash with golds and reds and oranges. I'd missed it, but the Spirit whispered that everything was okay. The Lord had a lesson to teach me—that peace can be found through Him and Him alone, even in the middle of a grand parade.

I started to laugh through my tears, and for a little while I felt the most powerful presence wrap peace and happiness around me. I laughed and laughed and had a distinct feeling Heavenly Father was in on the joke—not to make me the parade idiot, but to remind me that He is in charge. All my worries were His worries, too. I was not forgotten or abandoned.

I can't describe how I felt. It didn't last a long time, but the reality and intensity of that experience gave me the strength I needed to go home and face the challenges I needed to face, even though at that time I had no idea just how great they really were. God knew, and He was preparing me.

So my grand plan to go to the mountain had failed, but through God's love and His righteous sense of humor, He found me—even in the middle of a parade where I had no business being.

His Peace and Happiness

Oh, the lessons I have gleaned from that experience! We can never live the kind of life we want to live unless we know peace and happiness. I want to bear witness to you that as children of God we are not destined to be crushed by adversity or to mire ourselves in misery, but we are designed to be happy and at peace no matter the turmoil that boils around us.

It's clear to me now that God has a plan for us and that peace and happiness come only when we are absolutely confident that God is our caring Father, that Jesus is our ever-vigilant Shepherd, and that we are their sheep, numbered, named, and nurtured. We are part of God's fold, and when we are lost or injured and cry out to heaven through prayer and repentance, heaven will go to any length to bring us back safely if we get lost or injured.

As sheep in that holy fold, our peace and happiness are not defined by the world, whose definition attributes both peace and happiness to fortune, good luck, and pleasure. The source of our peace and happiness is not something we are handed, but something that we have already been given—a gift that must be opened from within us.

His Peace

When Jesus, Savior of the World, was preparing for His inevitable death, those closest to Him were understandably wrought with sorrow. I can only imagine the sadness Jesus' little fold must have suffered, listening to their Master testify of Himself and His Father, hearing Him promise that comfort would come, but that in "a little while" he would no longer be there to put an arm around them or to cheer them with a word or the smile that only He could offer (see John 14).

Among that group there was confusion. There was chaos. There was constant fear. Jesus did not condemn, but comforted. "My peace I give unto you: not as the world giveth, give I unto

you. Let not your heart be troubled, neither let it be afraid"
(John 14:27).

I used to take this scripture too lightly. I thought it was sweet
and that the admonishment was optional. I've changed my mind.
Though we can use our agency to reject this gift, I now know that
Jesus is not suggesting, but commanding our hearts to be at peace
and our lives to brim with happiness—no matter the circumstances.

Steps away from Gethsemane, moments away from the
greatest agony anyone born into mortality will ever face, Jesus
knelt in an upper room to wash the filthy feet of His disciples—
including those of Judas. At that time, there might have been a
bit of a pep talk to Himself in the Master's words: "In the world
ye shall have tribulation: but be of good cheer; I have overcome
the world" (John 16:33).

How our lives would change if when we are facing our greatest
trials we would kneel to wash the feet of others, if we would lift
up our heads and "be of good cheer," if we would proclaim, "I
have overcome!"

GOOD CHEER

Jesus would never command us to do something and fail to
provide the way for us to do it. If He says we can have peace and
happiness in the midst of tribulation, then we can. Jesus, who has
bequeathed to us His peace, *wants* and *expects* us to live lives that
reflect that reality. Over and over, His message is, "Be of good
cheer."

Speaking at a BYU Women's Conference, Camille Fronk
taught, "To the paralytic man lying helpless on a bed, Jesus
proclaimed, 'Be of good cheer' (Matthew 9:2). To the frightened

Apostles battling the tempestuous sea, Jesus appeared on the water, declaring, 'Be of good cheer' (Matthew 14:27). To Nephi the son of Nephi, who was subject to an arbitrary law threatening his life and the lives of other righteous Nephites if the signs prophesied by Samuel the Lamanite didn't occur, the Lord said, 'Lift up your head and be of good cheer' (3 Nephi 1:13). As Joseph Smith met with ten elders about to be sent out, two by two, to missions fraught with trouble and danger, the Lord announced, 'Be of good cheer' (D&C 61:36). In each instance the people had every reason to be anxious, fearful, and hopeless, yet the Lord directed them toward a reason to rejoice" ("'In the World Ye Shall Have Tribulation: But Be of Good Cheer; I Have Overcome the World,'" address given April 30, 2004).

Why do you think Jesus repeats Himself on this issue?

THE VERY PURPOSE OF OUR CREATION

When is the last time you were so happy you couldn't wipe the smile off your face? When is the last time you felt such peace that even an earthquake couldn't shake you? We are designed by a loving Father in Heaven to live in peace. Jesus Christ atoned so that our happiness can be lasting. "Adam fell that men might be; and men are, that they might have joy" (2 Ne. 2:25). "And the Messiah" came to "redeem the children of men from the fall" (2 Ne. 2:26).

The very reason we exist, the very reason we were created was made clear by the Prophet Joseph Smith: "Happiness is the object and design of our existence" (*Teachings of the Prophet Joseph Smith,* 255). President Lorenzo Snow said, "The Lord has not given us the gospel that we may go around mourning all the days of our lives" (in Joseph B. Wirthlin, "The Abundant Life," *Ensign,* May 2006, 99).

What makes me sad is that there are so many of us with the blessings and truths of the gospel, yet the circumstances in our lives keep us from experiencing peace and happiness. We slog through life with broken hearts and broken spirits, with heads that hang down and hearts that are heavy.

I have an absolutely beautiful friend who appears to have everything. She has a testimony, a family, a job, health, and financial security. In spite of everything, she is one of the least happy people I know. Whenever I ask her how she's doing, her reply is the same: "I'm just getting through one day at a time."

This life is too short to waste a single day! The world might just be going through one day at a time, but not us. We are defined by Christ, we know who He is, we know His plan, we know our true identity. No more dragging ourselves through life—it's time to live and to savor every minute, even those wrought with pain!

DEFINITION OF PEACE AND HAPPINESS

Some smart but anonymous person said, "Real peace is not only the absence of conflict, but also the presence of justice." For those who have been abused or betrayed, there is assurance in that statement, but true peace is greater than knowing God will be just and that there will be an absence of war. It is a tranquil state of not being shaken even when the storms of life rage around us. It's having Jesus as the anchor that holds us steady.

Living a peaceful life is something the scriptures don't just suggest, but admonish us to do. 1 Peter 3:11 makes it clear what our part in the deal is: "Let him eschew evil, and do good; let him seek peace, and ensue it." *Ensue* means to guarantee or to make certain of. Again, the Lord will never command us to do something and leave us no way to do it. Peace is a blessing we must actively seek and not give up until it is ours.

Happiness? It's that elusive state that everyone longs for. The best definition I could find was summed up in 4 Nephi: "And there were no envyings, nor strifes, nor tumults, nor whoredoms, nor lyings, nor murders, nor any manner of lasciviousness; and surely there could not be a happier people among all the people who had been created by the hand of God" (4 Ne. 1:16).

Why? "Because of the love of God which did dwell in the hearts of the people" (4 Ne. 1:15).

Elder James E. Talmage has said, "Happiness leaves no bad aftertaste, it is followed by no depressing reaction; it calls for no repentance, brings no regret, entails no remorse; pleasure too often makes necessary repentance, contrition, and suffering; and, if indulged to the extreme, it brings degradation and destruction.

"True happiness is lived over and over again in memory, always with a renewal of the original good; a moment of unholy pleasure may leave a barbed sting, which, like a thorn in the flesh, is an ever-present source of anguish.

"Happiness is not akin with levity, nor is it one with light-minded mirth. It springs from the deeper fountains of the soul, and is not infrequently accompanied by tears. Have you never been so happy that you have to weep? I have" (*Improvement Era*, 17:2, 173).

WHERE NOT TO FIND IT

Peace and happiness are within us. We'll never find them in a place or in a package. We'll never find them by whining or murmuring. We'll never find them as long as we are ungrateful, as long as we refuse to forgive, as long as we cling to bitterness, hatred, vengeance. They will not be found as we wallow in pity or any type of self-destructive behavior.

It's not our circumstances that determine our peace and happiness—it's our attitude toward those circumstances. It's how we choose to live in spite of what's going on around us. It's what's going on inside of us that counts most. Think about the children of Israel—there's a reason they are called "children." When they were hungry they murmured. When they were tired or uncomfortable, they blamed Moses for their troubles. They focused on what they *didn't have* instead of what they *had*—and when push came to shove, they got downright vicious. As they "murmured against Moses, [they] said, Wherefore is this that thou hast brought us up out of Egypt, to kill us and our children and our cattle with thirst?" (Ex. 17:3).

They were at the point of stoning Moses, when all he'd done was deliver them.

They forgot about the deliverance, though. And what was the reward for murmuring? It took forty years for them to make an eleven-day journey. Only the most valiant and positive made it to the Promised Land. The others camped, stayed put, and did not progress. They died without tasting the fruits of the Promised Land. No wonder Nephi told us to liken the scriptures unto ourselves!

It took a long time for me to finally realize that maybe the trials I was going through held a valuable lesson that I just wasn't willing to learn—and that perhaps the Lord let me stay camped out in the desert until I finally learned what He needed me to learn: We can choose to praise instead of murmur. We can choose to not live in bondage by ridding ourselves of anger, frustration, judgment, fear, guilt, and bitterness.

The Apostle Paul had a nagging "thorn" that he had to deal with. He chose to focus on Jesus instead and said his determined purpose was to "know him, and the power of his resurrection" (Phil. 3:10). The "thorn"—whatever it was—got only a mention, while the focus was a choice of attitude for Paul, who chose the better part.

Freedom, peace, and genuine happiness are found in forging a healthy relationship with ourselves. We'll never find peace and happiness in tearing ourselves down, in holding on to grudges against ourselves. We all mess up. You're not the only one who makes blunders—even big, bad blunders. I'd say losing 116 pages of the original Book of Mormon manuscript was a significant blunder, wouldn't you? The Lord told Joseph: "You should have been faithful; and [God] would have extended his arm and supported you against all the fiery darts of the adversary; and he would have been with you in every time of trouble" (D&C 3:8).

Wow. Can you imagine how Joseph felt?

Yet the Lord never chastens us to make us feel lousy, but to lead us to repentance. I love Joseph Smith for a lot of reasons, but one is his forthrightness. "I often felt condemned for my weakness and imperfections," he admitted (JS—H 1:29).

After winning one of the most dramatic battles against evil in all of scripture, the prophet Elijah fell into such a deep depression that he "went a day's journey into the wilderness, and came and sat down under a juniper tree: and he requested for himself that he might die; and said, It is enough; now, O Lord, take away my life" (1 Kgs. 19:4). Nephi takes us into the shadowy corner of his heart: "O wretched man that I am! Yea, my heart sorroweth because of my flesh; my soul grieveth because of mine iniquities" (2 Ne. 4:17).

It's wrong of us to think that Jesus does not know what sorrow or rejection feel like. He was "despised and rejected of men; a man of sorrows, and acquainted with grief: . . . and we esteemed him not" (Isa. 53:3).

These examples and more give us hope, because with God there is always hope.

After Joseph was proven penitent, imagine his joy when the Lord said, "Remember, God is merciful; therefore, repent of that which thou hast done which is contrary to the commandment which I gave you, and thou art still chosen" (D&C 3:10).

You might say, *Well, that was Joseph Smith. He was a prophet. I'm just an ordinary person.* But remember this: in God's economy, He does not esteem one flesh above another, but He "inviteth them all to come unto him and partake of his goodness; and he denieth none that come unto him, black and white, bond and free, male and female; . . . all are alike unto God" (2 Ne. 26:33).

Peace and happiness will *never* be found in sin. I don't care how alluring the packaging or the promise. When it falls from the tongue of the father of lies, it's a lie. As the Book of Mormon teaches: "wickedness never was happiness" (Alma 41:10). Truly, "despair cometh . . . of iniquity" (Moro. 10:22).

Today the devil plays a deadly game called *instant gratification.* The Lord tries us and stretches out our patience, but not Satan. He says do what feels good. Do what you want. Do it now. It will make you happy! As Latter-day Saints we know better. Elder James E. Faust made it clear when he taught that the instant gratification of all we want would be the most direct way to unhappiness (see "Our Search for Happiness," *Ensign,* Oct. 2000, 2).

There is a plan in place for when we sin. The devil will have us put off repentance, will try to convince us to hide our sins so we will not have to be embarrassed or ashamed or have to deal with the consequences. But the Lord, whose opinion matters most, already knows what we've done behind closed doors and in the darkest places of our hearts. We can hide nothing from Him. So I urge you to repent right away so that your life can be filled with peace and happiness. When we truly repent of our sins, the Lord promises, "I, the Lord, remember them no more" (D&C 58:42).

SIN GETS IN THE WAY

Sin and its subsequent regret can be our biggest obstacle to peace and happiness. David knew this and came before the Lord a soiled sinner, yet a faithful believer. He not only showed faith in God, but in himself, too: "Have mercy upon me, O God, according to thy lovingkindness: according unto the multitude of thy tender mercies blot out my transgressions. Wash me thoroughly from mine iniquity, and cleanse me from my sin. For I acknowledge my transgressions: and my sin is ever before me. . . . Purge me with hyssop, and I shall be clean: wash me, and I shall be whiter than snow. Make me to hear joy and gladness; that the bones which thou hast broken may rejoice. Hide thy face from my sins, and blot out all mine iniquities. Create in me a clean heart, O God; and renew a right spirit within me" (Ps. 51:1–3, 7–10).

When was the last time we prayed for the Lord to create in us a clean heart and a right spirit?

Maybe it's time.

Another effective prayer that we may fail to pray is to ask the Holy Ghost to tell us what we need to repent of. He makes known "the truth of all things" (Moro. 10:5), teaches all things and brings all things to one's remembrance (see John 14:26), and reproves the world of sin (see John 16:8). How can we begin to repent unless we acknowledge our sin? We can't. It's the first step to living a life that has been cleared and cleaned of sin.

Alma urged Corianton to understand this when he said, "Let your sins trouble you, with that trouble which shall bring you down unto repentance. . . . Do not endeavor to excuse yourself in the least point" (Alma 42:29–30).

You can't fake your way through repentance. Oh, you might fool your priesthood leaders, you might fool your loved ones, and you might even fool yourself. But you will never fool God. True repentance is the kind of repentance marked by godly sorrow that transforms lives. Paul wrote about this with power: "Now I rejoice, not that ye were made sorry, but that ye sorrowed to repentance: for ye were made sorry after a godly manner, that ye might receive damage by us in nothing. For godly sorrow worketh repentance to salvation not to be repented of: but the sorrow of the world worketh death" (2 Cor. 7:9–10).

Get Rid of the Guilt and Condemnation

Godly sorrow is a good thing. Guilt is not. I've learned that the Holy Ghost may convict us when we sin in order to prod us to repentance, but the Lord and His Spirit will never berate or belittle us. Guilt is used only to move us to repentance. Condemnation is not of Christ.

If I've sinned, I need to repent. I need to repent without delay, and I need to repent sincerely and completely. I need to recognize if what I am feeling is coming from the Lord or the devil. One encourages, one discourages.

There are a few buttons that can still be pushed to make us feel crushing guilt. President Hinckley pointed out that nothing will have as profound effect on us as the way our children turn out (see "'Great Shall Be the Peace of Thy Children'," *Ensign,* Nov. 2000, 50). But that sentiment raises feelings of guilt for my friend whose son drowned in the bathtub while she was in an adjoining room. No matter how much time passes, no matter how many words of comfort are whispered, she talks about the life her son would have had, how his future would have turned out . . . if only.

She beats herself up with every rising sun. Is that repentance? How does the Atonement of Christ work in her life? It doesn't. It breaks my heart to know the healing that is available to her, yet she refuses it because she feels guilty and unworthy.

It's for her I wrote this book.

It's for you.

It's for me.

Christ didn't just atone for our sins. He atoned for our mistakes. He atoned for our errors in judgment. He atoned for all that we do imperfectly.

WHERE TO FIND PEACE AND HAPPINESS

King Benjamin taught that "never-ending happiness" comes from keeping the commandments of God (Mosiah 2:41). "What is the price of happiness?" asked Spencer W. Kimball. "One might be surprised at the simplicity of the answer. The treasure house of happiness is unlocked to those who live the gospel of Jesus Christ in its purity and simplicity. Like a mariner without stars, like a traveler without a compass, is the person who moves along through life without a plan. The assurance of supreme happiness, the certainty of a successful life here and of exaltation and eternal life hereafter, come to those who plan to live their lives in complete harmony with the gospel of Jesus Christ—and then consistently follow the course they have set" (*The Miracle of Forgiveness,* [1969], 259).

Such a journey is made on stepping-stones of selflessness, wisdom, contentment, and faith. The enemies of progress and fulfillment are such things as self-doubt, a poor self-image, self-pity, bitterness, and despair. By substituting simple faith and humility for these enemies, we can move rapidly in our search for happiness.

FOLLOW THE LEADER

So many times—too many times—we see Jesus Christ depicted as a somber, solitary, and sad figure. He was acquainted with sorrow and grief, yet it is my personal witness that Jesus loved life! He knew peace in a tempest. He knew happiness and knew how to shed tears of joy! Liken the words of the resurrected Savior as He spoke to the Nephites: "Blessed are ye because of your faith. And now behold, my joy is full. And when he had said these words, he wept, and the multitude bare record of it, and he took their little children, one by one, and blessed them, and prayed unto the Father for them" (3 Ne. 17:20–21).

Think back to Lehi's dream. "As I partook of the fruit thereof it filled my soul with exceedingly great joy; wherefore, I began to be desirous that my family should partake of it also; for I knew that it was desirable above all other fruit" (1 Ne. 8:12). This tree produced fruit that "was desirable to make one happy" (1 Ne. 8:10). Hear the love that was evident when Lehi said, "as I partook of the fruit thereof it filled my soul with exceedingly great joy; wherefore, I began to be desirous that my family should partake of it also."

That's how our Heavenly Father feels about us! He wants us to partake of all He has, all He is, and all that leads to peace and happiness. He wants above all else that we "prosper and be in health, even as [our] soul prospereth" (see 3 Jn. 1:2). He wants us to have all that we can have and still keep Him first in our lives. Sometimes we think we want things, not knowing that they will interfere in our relationship with God. Let nothing come between you and your Father in Heaven. Nothing. No one.

Don't Spend—Invest

"Every aspect of the gospel of Jesus Christ—the principles, the doctrines, and the commandments—is a part of our Heavenly Father's plan to help us obtain peace and happiness" (Joseph B. Wirthlin, "Three Choices," *Liahona,* Nov. 2003, 78). We only have one chance to get life right. We know who we are, we know why we are here, and we *know* that peace and happiness are gifts God has already given us. They are found within us as we live the gospel.

The devil knows that, too. He will provide plenty of people to make you miserable—people who judge, criticize, and reject. When you are confident about who you are in Christ, you can say, "I'd like you to accept me, but if you reject me, I'll be okay, because God is on my side."

You can smile through the tears. You can choose to say to the devil, "I'm not going to live with a sprit of fear and dread and regret. I'm going to repent, and God will put in me a clean heart and a right spirit. I'm going to know peace and live a life of genuine happiness. It's part of the plan, so get behind me, Satan, because, like Paul, I'm forgetting what lies behind and I am moving forward."

Don't waste a single second in self-pity or self-destruction. Don't *spend* your time; learn to *invest* it. Try new things. Love people. Reach out and share your peace and happiness with others who are lost in darkness and pain.

Isn't it great that no matter how dismal our circumstances are, they do not dictate the quality of our lives? Our attitude dictates the quality of our lives—and we *choose* our attitude.

No matter how dark our circumstances are, we can say, "I'm not going to live with a spirit of guilt and condemnation." When Satan tells you that life is hopeless, you can tell yourself with confidence that the Savior will safely lead you over the most difficult obstacles of life and that as you navigate through this world clinging to Him, you will find peace and happiness (see Richard G. Scott, "The Atonement Can Secure Your Peace and Happiness," *Liahona,* Nov. 2006, 40).

What brings you peace?

What makes you happy?

Peace comes from knowing that we are living the commandments to the best of our ability. Peace comes in the assurance that when we mess up, there is a way to be good again. That way is Jesus Christ. He is the *only* way. Happiness comes as we forget ourselves and learn to serve others.

I find my happiest moments are spent with those I love, my family and my friends. It doesn't take much to make me happy—just a smile or a kind word. Peace comes when I let go of pain and turn my burden over to Christ's capable arms.

Peace comes in knowing that we are not alone, even though the devil tells us that we are.

Although we exist that we "might have joy" (2 Ne. 2:25), this does not mean our lives will always be filled with joy, for by divine design "there is an opposition in all things" (2 Ne. 2:11). Knowing this allows me to cut depression off at the pass. When hard times come, I say aloud, "Help me to hurry and learn what I need to learn from this experience so that I can move forward!"

LOVE

If you combined peace and happiness, I think the result would be love, the kind of love the Savior of mankind exhibited every day of His life. As you learn to love as He loves, you will soar above the ill winds that blow, above the sordid, the self-defeating, and the bitter. You have the promise that "your whole bodies shall be filled with light, and there shall be no darkness in you; and that body which is filled with light comprehendeth all things" (D&C 88:67).

One of my all-time favorite sentiments from President Thomas S. Monson tells us what makes him happy: the feeling that the Lord answered someone's prayer through him. What an expression of great love!

WE NEED THE GOSPEL

There are countless counterfeits, but there is only *one* "great plan of happiness" (Alma 42:8). It is the gospel of Jesus Christ.

You want to know how to be truly and lastingly happy and at peace? There is no other way except the Lord's way. Let's continue the quote from Joseph Smith that began this chapter: "Happiness is the object and design of our existence; and will be the end thereof, if we pursue the path that leads to it; and this path is virtue, uprightness, faithfulness, holiness, and keeping all the commandments of God" (*Teachings of the Prophet Joseph Smith*, 255–56). "I would desire that ye should consider on the blessed and happy state of those that keep the commandments of God.

For behold, they are blessed in all things, both temporal and spiritual; and if they hold out faithful to the end they are received into heaven, that thereby they may dwell with God in a state of never-ending happiness" (Mosiah 2:41).

Travel back with me to that autumn day in Payson. The good citizens of Payson know how to find a reason to celebrate. They throw a parade in honor of onions! I love it! Picture the parade route and all the gleeful spectators. Imagine the blare of the bands and the shouts from the royalty. Hear the click of the high-stepping horse hooves against the asphalt. Feel the excitement. See me slumped way, way down behind my steering wheel, embarrassed beyond belief.

How could the Lord take a situation like that and teach me about peace and happiness?

Because He is the Lord of peace and happiness.

Peace isn't an emotion; it's a foundation. Happiness isn't a feeling; it's a state of being. You can't travel to a place and find it—because it's not *where* you are, it's *how* you are. It's recognizing when you have become part of something greater than yourself. Then that moment becomes a memory that you can revisit and reexperience. The memory brings back the emotions, the peace, and the happiness.

For me, it came after the parade when I felt the Savior's assurance that He was mindful of me. Sometimes when I hear a tuba blow or slice into an onion, I remember a sense of peace and happiness that makes me smile. It makes no sense to anyone except me and Christ, and that's okay. I smile anyway.

After all the things that can be said about peace and happiness, let me leave you with this one summation by a prophet of God: "You will find peace and happiness if you live the gospel" (Gordon B. Hinckley, "Inspirational Thoughts," *Ensign*, Aug. 1997, 3).

TRUTH #7:
Good Trumps Evil

I am come that they might have life,
and that they might have it more abundantly.
—John 10:10

I wish I could sit with you, look into your eyes, and testify to you that your life does not have to be defined by anyone except Jesus Christ. I wish I could hold you in my arms and promise you how much you are loved and needed, that you are never alone, and that if you will just hang in there with everything you've got, you will come off triumphant! It's my prayer that you will feel my faith and my love through the power of these pages.

I initially wrote this book because my own heart was broken and I had to know the truth about God, about Jesus, and about myself. As it came together all I could think about were the people I knew who were also broken and hurting and who needed to know what I was learning.

The Lord made it simple for me. First we hurt, then we heal, and then we help other people who are hurting.

Quickly, let's review the whole process of letting Christ define us. First, we are children of the Most High God. He is our spiritual Father and that means we have His spiritual DNA. He wants us to become like Him, to live the eternal life that He lives, to inherit all that He has—and He has everything. We are loved beyond measure by our Father. And as children of God, our worth is infinite.

Jesus Christ is our Savior. He is not some distant god who is quick and harsh to punish. The Savior I have come to know is involved, patient, and "mighty to save" (2 Ne. 31:19). There is no overestimating the value of Christ in our lives. It's His voice that needs to be the definitive voice we listen to.

There is a plan in place. Elder Richard G. Scott assured us that in an uncertain world, there are two things, among others, that will never change: the profound love our Heavenly Father has for us, and the fact that there is a plan in place—a plan that leads the way to happiness (see "The Power of a Strong Testimony," *Liahona,* Jan. 2002, 100–103).

We know, too, that Satan is out to destroy us. Remember what my friend says: "There are only two times Satan will come against us—when we are doing what's wrong and when we are doing what's right." In other words, as long as we are living, Satan will be after our souls.

In spite of adversity, peace and happiness lie within us. Each of us, regardless of our circumstances, can live a remarkable, rewarding life. We really define the quality of our lives by the everyday decisions we make—not based solely on circumstances, but based on our attitudes toward those circumstances.

We are designed to succeed. "And when we obtain any blessing from God, it is by obedience to that law upon which it is predicated" (D&C 130:21). The Lord wants each one of us to be a success. All we need to do is to find out the law governing that success and then go forward from there. Sterling W. Sill once said that "the most exciting experience we can have in mortality is to have a high rating in that important enterprise in which God himself spends his entire time: the salvation of mankind" ("The One Business of Life," *Ensign,* Jan. 1981, 51).

Even if we have made a significant mess of our lives, Christ's power can take our messes and turn them into His messages. There is hope through Christ for redefining our lives if they need it. No more excuses. We have the right to live the quality lives that Christ wants us to live.

So we come to the point when we must practice what we preach. We must liken what we've learned. We must live what we believe!

Go ahead—pick up the scriptures. Read to the end of the book—good trumps evil.

Stay on the Lord's side and you're guaranteed a victory, because our Heavenly Father is greater and has greater power than anything Satan is or anything he has.

But how do we stay on the Lord's side when life is so difficult and wrought with so many landmines? How do we stay strong when life relentlessly batters us? I have learned that the first decision we make when we feel pain will determine how deep that pain goes and how long the pain lasts.

When we hurt, do we turn to the Lord? Or do we think we have to suffer alone? Do we think we have to pay the price? Or do we turn to a loving Savior who has paid the price for us?

HURT

Not long ago I drove to Las Vegas in a car packed with teenaged boys. As we entered "Sin City" we were visually bombarded with images and written words that were offensive to the Spirit. Billboards rose up like screeching demons. Then we saw one single billboard that stood alone. It read: *If Christ Be For You, Who Can Be Against You?*

That's it.

Those boys noted that sign and talked about it over and over. If Christ is on our side, no matter the assault, we will come out winners. This assurance should help us endure the difficult times with strength and patience.

When I was twelve years old, I was in foster care. I lived on a farm. For a city girl who adores animals, that was a real treat. Along the shoreline of the river, wild geese nested. I found one nest stuffed with eggs. Outside the perimeter of dried grass and downy feathers was a single egg that had rolled away. Of course I rescued it.

I was a little bit like Dr. Seuss's Horton—I took it upon myself to hatch that egg. Everyone laughed at me as I carried it back to my bedroom, as I placed a bare light bulb above it, and as I wrapped it in a warm heating pad. I loved that egg. I talked to it, I sang to it, I prayed over it. I rolled it gently and loved it desperately. I slept beside it, for pity sakes!

After a few weeks I was rewarded with the tiniest crack in the shell. I put my ear to the egg and heard a faint peeping noise. My heart burst with happiness! I was going to be a mother goose!

I've got tears on my cheeks now, just remembering how happy I was as that little goose began to peck its way into this world. At first, all I could see was a little beak. Then some wet grayish-yellow down.

The poor thing, I thought, as it struggled and struggled to break free of that hard, giant shell. I tried to be patient, really I did. But I was alone with my gosling. It was the middle of the night, and my heart ached for the struggle the pitiful thing was going through. It would chirp and peck, then it would go still and rest. I was afraid the struggle would kill it. So I did what I thought was the right thing to do: I took my fingernail and began to break the shell for the gosling.

I can't drag this story out. It's too painful. I broke the rest of the shell for that little bird, and then I cupped its damp, warm body in the palm of my hand. It was the most precious thing in the world to me, and I watched its little heart beat up and down, up and down, up and down, then down and not back up.

It died in my hands.

You see, that little bird did not have the strength to live because I had deprived it of its struggle. God had designed the shell to be hard, but not so hard the bird could not break through with great effort. God had it all figured out—how the struggle would provide the strength for that bird's best chance at life. I'd taken away the struggle, and the bird did not have the strength to survive.

Because I meddled, I cost that precious little gosling its life.

Are you getting the message?

There are times, in God's wisdom, when our strength comes from our struggle. If we don't do our part, exert our faith and energy, He is not going to step in and do His part to rescue us, because that would not be best for us.

It's all part of God's great design. If we weren't equipped to handle the hurt, God would not expect us to survive it. When we hurt, and the struggle seems too great, when fear comes upon us, the definitive voice tells us that He has "not given us the spirit of fear; but of power, and of love, and of a sound mind" (2 Tim. 1:7). Love means loving our God, others, and ourselves. Power comes from living what we learn. A sound mind results when we know the difference between what the world says and what God says. It's what this book is all about.

Everyone hurts.

Some of that pain is physical; other times it's mental or spiritual. It results from our own actions and from the actions of others. Pain is pain. It's part of life, but as long as we cling to our pain and let it define our lives, as long as we swim in it, we will never get to the shore.

We are not addressing physical pain here, but the spiritual agony that we all suffer. In the beginning of this book I told you that I used to think that Heavenly Father looked down on me with disappointment and disapproval. I used to think I'd failed Him, and that thought caused me to writhe in pain.

Guess what? Heavenly Father is not shocked or surprised or disappointed in us. If any truth should heal our wounded spirits, it is knowing, as Elder Jeffrey R. Holland told us, that our Heavenly Father is much more merciful than we would ever believe (see "The Grandeur of God," *Liahona,* Nov. 2003, 70–73).

I don't know the pain you're going through, but your Heavenly Father knows. His Son stands ready to heal you everywhere you hurt. But you have to come to Him. You have to ask, to knock, to seek. As Dr. Martin Luther King advised, "Take the first step in faith. You don't have to see the whole staircase, just take the first step."

I don't worry much about the future. I've found that living the best life I can live means living the moment I'm in to the fullest. If you feel deprived or anxious, take heart from what various prophets have taught: that everything we are denied in this life will be made up to us in the next.

If your days seem dark, even when the sun shines for the rest of the world, take heart in what Elder Jeffrey R. Holland taught:

that even if you can't always see the "silver lining" in your clouds, your Heavenly Father can, and He will match your tears with His own as He provides the light you are seeking (see "'An High Priest of Good Things to Come'," *Ensign,* Nov. 1999, 36).

HEALING

Thirty-eight years.

That's how long the hurting man at the pools of Bethesda waited to get healed.

Thirty-eight years is a long time. Maybe even long enough to wiggle your way to the water's edge. But that's not what happened, and when Jesus came to the pools of Bethesda, there "lay a great multitude of impotent folk, of blind, halt, withered, waiting for the moving of the water. For an angel went down at a certain season into the pool, and troubled the water: whosoever then first after the troubling of the water stepped in was made whole of whatsoever disease he had. And a certain man was there, which had an infirmity thirty and eight years. When Jesus saw him lie, and knew that he had been now a long time in that case, he saith unto him, Wilt thou be made whole? The impotent man answered him, Sir, I have no man, when the water is troubled, to put me into the pool: but while I am coming, another steppeth down before me. Jesus saith unto him, Rise, take up thy bed, and walk. And immediately the man was made whole, and took up his bed, and walked" (John 5:3–9).

What was the first question Jesus asked the man? *Wilt thou be made whole? Do you want to get well?*

I can almost hear the tone in the man's voice as he says, "Sir, I have no man, when the water is troubled, to put me into the pool."

How many of us make the excuse that we are all alone and have no one to help us?

We all have excuses to keep hurting, but we are not meant to live lives of pain and suffering. We are meant to be made whole and for our healing to reflect God's goodness and power. How can His light shine through us when we live in shadow and suffering? It can't.

Next the man suggests blame like so many of us have a tendency to do: "but while I am coming, another steppeth down before me."

There will always be people who get in our way. No more excuses!

Jesus, the voice that never dwells on the problem, but presents the answer, said, "Rise, take up thy bed, and walk."

He knew the man's heart. He read the man's faith.

He knows your heart. He reads your faith.

When we come to the Lord for healing, are we willing to "get up," "move," and "clean up our mess"? The scriptures tell us to "Examine yourselves, whether ye be in the faith; prove your own selves" (2 Cor. 13:5).

Onward and upward should always be our direction. We can't be faithless; we can't be timid. If we are serious about getting healed, we have to be faithful and firm. Our God is plain, clear, and specific. Our prayers should be that way. Our lives should be that way.

There is no minimizing your pain. If you need professional help to heal, get that help! Don't delay and don't make excuses. Find someone you can trust in whom to confide. But know this: you can always confide in your Father in Heaven. No one knows you better or cares about you more.

I used to feel pain that I did not have the same foundation as others around me. I don't feel that way anymore. An article I found in a past edition of the *Ensign* gave me a healthy perspective on how I view life's experiences. After telling of the horrific and painful circumstances in which she had found herself, the author rejoiced in the fact that those experiences had made her the person she is (see Mildred Barthel, "Happiness along the Way," *Ensign,* Apr. 1987, 42).

I promise you there is healing through the power of Christ's Atonement. It heals every kind of pain there is. It stops the bleeding, and though you may have scars, they are reminders of how good the Master Physician is—how skilled—because they are there to remind us that something bad happened a long time ago. They remind us that the memory can be brought back, but not the pain. As President James E. Faust taught, the basic source of the soul's healing is the Atonement of Jesus Christ (see "The Atonement: Our Greatest Hope," *Ensign,* Nov. 2001, 18).

Healing doesn't always involve removing the wound. Sometimes we have to live with it, but God makes it bearable.

Whether we are healed or not, we must stay true to the course we set out on so long ago. There is power and peace in obedience that can never be found in any other place.

Isn't that a wonderful way to embrace life? All the good, the bad, and the ugly make us who we are and make us compassionate and empathetic and more useful in the hands of God to reach out and hold and help others to heal.

The process of healing is just that—a process. President Marion G. Romney equated it with the process of conversion and said that one "may be assured of it when by the power of the Holy Spirit his soul is healed. When this occurs, he will recognize it by the way he feels, for he will feel as the people of Benjamin felt when they received remission of sins. The record says, '. . . the Spirit of the Lord came upon them, and they were filled with joy, having received a remission of their sins, and having peace of conscience. . .' (Mosiah 4:3)" (*Conference Report,* Oct. 1963, 25).

Help

We've talked a lot about the love that God has for us, but what about the love we have for Him? The Prophet Joseph Smith taught us that "the nearer we get to our heavenly Father, the more we are disposed to look with compassion on perishing souls; we feel that we want to take them upon our shoulders, and cast their sins behind our backs" (*Teachings of the Prophet Joseph Smith,* 241).

"For how knoweth a man the master whom he has not served, and who is a stranger unto him, and is far from the thoughts and intents of his heart?" (Mosiah 5:13)

It's in helping that we begin to define our own lives.

When we know what it is to feel hurt and pain, when we know what it is to have the Savior of mankind sit beside us and comfort us until we have healed, then we have an obligation to go forward to help others who suffer as we once suffered.

William Wordsworth believed that a person's life is defined by "his little, nameless, unremembered acts of kindness and love." Those little, nameless, unremembered acts of kindness and love don't just happen. I learned this one day as I was hurrying to an appointment in Manhattan. My teenaged daughter was with me, and I was rushing down the sidewalk, encouraging her to keep pace. Somewhere along the trek I looked back and discovered she was no longer right behind me.

Of course I panicked. Suddenly the appointment did not seem so important. I ran, backtracking through the crowds, and discovered my daughter kneeling beside a homeless man, digging change out of her pockets to put into his outstretched hand.

The scene really touched me, and I stopped in my tracks to watch a precious exchange between a needy beggar and a teenage girl.

Later when she was safe in my arms I told her that I'd walked right past that man and hadn't even seen him. "How?" I asked her, "how did you even see him?"

She looked at me and smiled. "I was looking for someone to help, Mom."

We all need to look for someone to help, to be actively engaged in helping our brothers and sisters, no matter where they are or who they are. How we treat others is what will ultimately define our lives.

Think of the example Joseph Smith set in the line of service. When he called Brother John E. Page to go on a mission to Canada, Brother Page did what most of us do: he found an excuse. "Brother Joseph, I can't go to Canada. I don't have a coat to wear." What did the Prophet do? He took off his own coat, handed it to John Page, and said, "Wear this, and the Lord will bless you."

John Page went on his mission to Canada. Two years later he'd walked close to five thousand miles and baptized six hundred converts.

When Lyman O. Littlefield was thirteen years old he was part of Zion's Camp; as the camp entered Missouri, Lyman Littlefield had an encounter with the Prophet Joseph, of which he later wrote: "The journey was extremely toilsome for all, and the physical suffering, coupled with the knowledge of the persecutions endured by our brethren whom we were traveling to succor, caused me to lapse one day into a state of melancholy. As the camp was making ready to depart I sat tired and brooding by the roadside. The Prophet was the busiest man of the camp; and yet when he saw me, he turned from the great press of other duties to say a word of comfort to a child. Placing his hand upon my head, he said, 'Is there no place for you, my boy? If not, we must make one.' This circumstance made an impression upon my mind which long lapse of time and cares of [later] years have not effaced" (in George Q. Cannon, *Life of Joseph Smith the Prophet* [Salt Lake City: Deseret Book Company, 1986], 344).

One day, a group of eight African-Americans arrived at the Prophet's home in Nauvoo. They had traveled from their home in Buffalo, New York, some eight hundred miles away, so they could be with the prophet of God and with the Saints. Although they were free, they were forced to hide from those who might mistake them for runaway slaves. They endured cold and hardship, wearing out shoes and then socks until they walked on bare feet all the way to the City of Joseph.

When they arrived in Nauvoo, the Prophet welcomed them into his home and helped each of them find a place to stay. But there was one, a girl named Jane, who did not have a place to go, and she wept, not knowing what to do.

"We won't have tears here," Joseph said to her. He turned to Emma and said, "Here's a girl who says she [doesn't have a] home. Don't you think she has a home here?"

Emma agreed. From that day on, Jane Manning lived as a member of the family.

Years after the Prophet's martyrdom and after she had joined the pioneers and made the long trek to Utah, Jane Manning

James said that sometimes she would still "wake up in the middle of the night, and just think about Brother Joseph and Sister Emma and how good they [were] to me. Joseph Smith," she said, "was the finest man I ever saw on Earth." [George Q. Cannon, *Life of Joseph Smith the Prophet* [Salt Lake City: Deseret Book Company, 1986]

On another occasion, Sheriff Thomas King of Adams County and several others were sent as a posse to arrest the Prophet and deliver him to the emissaries of Governor Boggs of Missouri. Sheriff King became deathly ill, and the Prophet took the sheriff to his home in Nauvoo and nursed him like a brother for four days (Cannon, 372). Small, kind, and yet significant acts of service were not occasional for the Prophet.

How can we know if we are allowing Christ to define our lives, if we are following in His footsteps? Elder Marvin J. Ashton said the best and surest indicator is in how we treat others (see "The Tongue Can Be a Sharp Sword," *Ensign*, May 1992, 18).

A QUALITY LIFE

What kind of life do you want to live?

God has equipped you with everything you need to build an ideal life, but you will have to be daring. You're going to have to dare to stand alone, dare to be different, dare to reach out, and dare to be the one who lifts someone else. You can't be complacent or conform if you want to be an instrument in building God's kingdom.

For years I wanted to lose weight. It didn't matter how badly I desired to lose weight. It didn't matter how hard I prayed to lose weight. Nothing changed until I got up and got moving, until I did all I could do, to be mindful of what I did and didn't put into my mouth. No one else could lift the weights for me or hike the mountain or run the track. They could run beside me, but I had to run my own race. Until my attitude changed, my body stayed the same.

If you don't like the life you are living, only you can change it. I'm not talking about the circumstances, because sometimes they cannot be changed, but you *can* change your attitude. You can choose to be excellent, to take care of the body God has given to temple your spirit; you can take care of your mind and learn new things and develop new skills; you can take care of the people in your life and cherish them and serve them. You can learn new things and challenge yourself. You can move in a right direction.

You can choose to be grateful—to reach out to someone who is more lonely than you are. You can make a new friend. Learn a new skill. Brigham Young counseled that we should not "narrow ourselves up" in our learning, and he stressed that before us lies "eternity, with all its sparkling intelligence, lofty aspirations, and unspeakable glories" (*Journal of Discourses,* 8:9).

Everyday chores can become adventures if you approach them with that attitude. Share your testimony. Repent fast and furiously when you fail. Forgive quickly and completely. Meet new people, reconnect with old friends, try new foods, extend a challenge to yourself. It's fun to reach out and see how far God can stretch that reach.

This is our one shot at life. As long as we are still breathing, there is hope to create the quality of life that God wants us to live. There is no time to waste. We have choices to make, choices that carry eternal consequences, but we are within an allotted time frame called mortality in which to make those choices.

How do we choose wisely?

Defined By You

"William George Jordan once said, 'Man has two creators, his God and himself. The first creator furnishes him the raw materials of his life—the laws and conformity with which he can make that life what he will. The second creator—himself—has powers he rarely realizes. It is what a man makes of himself that counts'" (Marvin J. Ashton, "Be a Quality Person," *Ensign,* Feb. 1993, 64).

We decide what we make of ourselves with every decision that we make.

I can promise you this much—God is going to win in the end, but we can choose to win now. We can define the quality of our lives by relying on Christ first, last, and always. We don't need to feel sorrow that our works aren't as good or complete as we'd like. As King Benjamin taught, even after our best efforts, we are all still "unprofitable servants," but we can come to Christ through *His* good works.

Satan does not want us to understand our divine potential. He wants to confuse us and make us doubt ourselves and our Savior. But the Lord has given us scriptures and prophets and promptings to help us remember who we are. When Helaman lovingly spoke to his sons, Nephi and Lehi, he begged them to remember who they were and to let Christ define their lives: "And now, my sons, remember, remember that it is upon the rock of our Redeemer, who is Christ, the Son of God, that ye must build your foundation; that when the devil shall send forth his mighty winds, yea, his shafts in the whirlwind, yea, when all his hail and his mighty storm shall beat upon you, it shall have no power over you to drag you down to the gulf of misery and endless wo, because of the rock upon which ye are built, which is a sure foundation, a foundation whereon if men build they cannot fall" (Hel. 5:12).

We are hitting and pitching for the Lord's team, the team that is sure to win in the end. The Prophet Joseph Smith promised, "No unhallowed hand can stop the work from progressing; persecutions may rage, mobs may combine, armies may assemble, calumny may defame, but the truth of God will go forth boldly, nobly, and independent, till it has penetrated every continent, visited every clime, swept every country, and sounded in every ear, till the purposes of God shall be accomplished, and the Great Jehovah shall say the work is done" (*History of the Church,* 4:540).

You and I are part of that vision and promise. Long ago we made sacred vows to do just what we are doing—live in mortality, struggle to make right choices, take advantage of Christ's gift to us, and help each other along the way.

No relationship is more important than the one we forge with our Savior, because it determines the relationship we have with ourselves. Those relationships are built through the defining moments of our lives.

Certainly one of Joseph Smith's defining moments was when he chose to care for his jailer. Peter's was when he got out of the boat. Mary's was when she said, "be it unto me according to thy word" (Luke 1:38). Adam's was when he said, "I know not, save the Lord commanded me" (Moses 5:6). Noah's was when he picked up the hammer and started to build an ark while the sun was still shining. Nephi's was when he picked up the sword of Laban.

What will your defining moment be? You can't stage it. You can't forge it. You have to be ready when it comes.

Perhaps one of your defining moments will be when you let go and let God define your worth and destiny. I beg you—don't bludgeon yourself over your past sins and mistakes and failures. Repent and forgive yourself. Let Christ and Christ alone define your worth and destiny.

Jesus asked questions to make us think, to urge us to use our agency to define ourselves. "What think ye of Christ?" is the question that we must all answer while in the presence of the Savior.

Your defining moment, and mine, will be how we live to answer that question.

If you've made mistakes, like all of us have, know this: With Christ, it's never too late for a do-over. The catalyst for this book was the turning of that question into this: "What does Christ think of you?"

Now you know.

So put the book down. Fall to your knees. Pray to let Christ and Christ alone define your worth so you can see the blinding brilliance of your future.